HOW TO FINALLY START YOUR BUSINESS

The easy step-by-step guide to starting and managing your LLC without the stress

M. Schultz

Table of contents

INTRODUCTION

"No, I can't approve your time off to get married."

"I'm sorry, what?" I responded, flustered and in disbelief.

"Your requested time off is during our big semi-annual sale," my manager replied.

I wish I could say I reacted politely to the absurdity of those words, calmly articulating the importance of taking this time off. Instead, I did the opposite. After causing a scene in front of my co-workers (and possibly a few customers—I was too distressed to notice), my store manager finally decided to "work with me" and give me the entire week off. However, it could only be from Sunday to Saturday, not the Wednesday to Wednesday I had requested.

"Oh," I responded curtly. "So you're allowing me to take the entire week off starting Sunday so I can drive back on Saturday to prepare for work the next day—on my WEDDING DAY?! I'm getting married on a Saturday! I'm not driving back from Indiana to Florida on my wedding night just to work the next day!" I exclaimed.

I don't recall much of what was said after that. I was too distraught. Suffice it to say, I quit my job soon after that conversation.

This moment is just one of many from the toxic workplaces I've endured throughout my career. I knew I wanted—no, I had to—work for myself.

When I first toyed with the idea of launching my own business, I remember staring blankly at the maze of legal documents required for forming an LLC. The regulations and fear of making costly mistakes felt overwhelming. Like many of you, I was stepping into unfamiliar territory, armed only with a dream and an unyielding drive to succeed. But navigating the complexities of business structures and legal jargon was not part of that dream. This initial confusion and stress became my companions on the entrepreneurial path, a journey that many of you might be contemplating or have already embarked upon.

Over the years, I've navigated the choppy waters of managing small businesses and carved out a space for myself in the world of entrepreneurship. My experiences have not only taught me the ins and outs of business management but have also ignited a passion for making this journey smoother and more comprehensible for others. This book is the culmination of everything I've learned, structured to help you approach the formation and management of an LLC with confidence and a smile.

The aim here is simple: to demystify the process of starting and managing your own LLC. Whether you're a budding entrepreneur or a seasoned business owner looking to expand your knowledge, this book is designed for you.

This book promises to guide you through each step of your entrepreneurial journey with confidence. I've tailored this guide not only to educate but also to entertain, ensuring that the learning process is as enjoyable as it is informative.

Crafted specifically for aspiring business owners and small business managers, this book addresses those who recognize the value of structuring their ventures as LLCs but feel daunted by the perceived complexities. Each chapter is designed to build your understanding from the ground up, covering everything from the legal foundations to the day-to-day management of a thriving business, all presented in an easy-to-digest manner, free from overwhelming technical jargon.

As we progress, I encourage you to engage fully with the content, exercises, and additional resources provided. This journey is not just about reading; it's about doing, planning, and preparing to take tangible steps toward realizing your business aspirations. By the end of this book, you will be equipped not only with knowledge but also with practical tools to establish and grow your LLC.

Let's embark on this journey together—not just as a means to achieve financial freedom, but as a path toward fulfilling your personal aspirations and becoming your own boss. Remember, every significant achievement begins with the decision to try. Let this book be your first step toward that exciting and rewarding leap into entrepreneurship.

CHAPTER ONE

Laying the Groundwork

Every great business starts with a spark—an idea that ignites passion and invites potential. However, not every idea is ready for the marketplace. As an entrepreneur, your challenge is not just to dream but to align that dream with the realities of the market and regulatory environments.

This chapter will guide you through the essential first steps of molding your initial concept into a viable business model, ensuring that your LLC is not merely a legal entity but a profitable and sustainable venture. Here, we will explore how to evaluate your business idea against the critical criteria of market demand, personal alignment, scalability, and legal considerations. By addressing these foundational aspects, you set the stage for a business that excites you while meeting a real need in the marketplace.

Choosing the Right Business Idea for Your LLC

Assessing Market Viability

The cornerstone of any successful business is a product or service that meets a clear market need. Understanding this, your first task is to conduct thorough market research. This process goes beyond simply confirming that potential customers exist for your product; it requires a nuanced analysis of who these customers are, what they genuinely need, and how your competitors are currently meeting—or failing to meet—these needs.

Begin by identifying your potential customer base and segmenting it by demographics, behaviors, and preferences. This segmentation will provide a clearer picture of your target audience and help you tailor your offerings effectively.

Next, evaluate your competitors with a critical eye. Examine their products, pricing, marketing strategies, and customer feedback. What are they doing well, and where do they fall short? This information is invaluable—not only for positioning your product but also for identifying the unique value proposition that makes your business stand out. Remember, a viable market isn't just about having many potential customers; it's about understanding those customers so well that you can serve them better than anyone else.

Aligning with Personal Passion and Expertise

While market demand is critical, a successful business must also resonate personally with you, the entrepreneur. Your passion and expertise will fuel the long hours and drive innovation. Reflect on what you are passionate about and where your strengths lie. Consider how these can be transformed into a business model. For instance, if you have a background in technology and a passion for education, an ed-tech startup might be the perfect avenue. This alignment not only increases your chances of persevering during tough times but also imbues your business with authenticity—a quality that today's consumers highly value.

Evaluating Scalability and Growth Potential

Before committing to a business idea, it's crucial to understand its scalability. Can this business grow in its current market, or can it expand into new markets? Factors to consider include market trends, potential barriers to entry, and the scalability of your production or service delivery model. For example, if you're launching a product-based business, do you have reliable suppliers who can scale with you? If it's a service-based business, can the service be standardized or automated to handle increased demand? Understanding these factors will help you gauge the long-term potential of your business idea and plan for sustainable growth.

Considering Legal and Regulatory Implications

Finally, any business idea must be examined through the lens of legal and regulatory frameworks, particularly when forming an LLC. Some industries are heavily regulated, impacting how quickly you can bring a product to market or expand operations. For instance, if you're entering the healthcare sector, patient privacy laws and medical regulations will significantly shape your business practices. Consulting with a legal expert at this stage can provide critical insights into the specific regulations you need to comply with and how they might affect your business model. This understanding is crucial to avoid costly legal mistakes and ensure your business operates smoothly within its legal boundaries.

By methodically analyzing these four critical areas—competitors, personal passion, scalability, and legal implications—you lay a solid foundation for your business. This initial groundwork not only aids in making informed decisions but also sets the stage for the detailed planning and strategic execution that will follow in the subsequent chapters of this book.

Understanding the Legal Structure of an LLC

Navigating the legalities of business ownership can be daunting, but understanding the structure of a Limited Liability Company (LLC) is crucial for leveraging its benefits. At the heart of its appeal is the principle of limited liability, which safeguards an owner's personal assets—such as bank accounts, homes, and other possessions—from business debts and liabilities.

Imagine a scenario where your business faces a lawsuit claiming damages that exceed the company's current assets. In a sole proprietorship, personal assets can be seized to cover the shortfall. However, an LLC provides a protective barrier; only the assets within the company can be targeted, leaving your personal holdings untouched. This protection not only offers peace of mind but also encourages an entrepreneurial spirit by mitigating personal risk.

Distinctions Between LLCs and Other Business Entities

When comparing an LLC to other business entities, several key distinctions emerge. Unlike a sole proprietorship or a general partnership, where owners bear unlimited liability for business debts, an LLC offers liability protection while maintaining operational flexibility. In contrast to corporations, which are required to adhere to stringent operational procedures—including regular board meetings and recorded minutes—an LLC enjoys a more flexible management structure. This flexibility is often appealing to small business owners who prefer less formality.

Additionally, the tax treatment of an LLC can be more advantageous. While corporations face double taxation on dividends (taxed at both corporate and individual levels), LLCs benefit from pass-through taxation, meaning profits are taxed only once at the member's personal income level. This tax efficiency, coupled with operational flexibility and liability protection, makes LLCs a preferred choice for many new businesses.

Management Structure of an LLC

The flexibility in management structure within an LLC warrants careful consideration. You can choose between a member-managed or a manager-managed LLC. In a member-managed LLC, all members (owners) participate in the decision-making processes of the business.

This arrangement is suitable for smaller, more collaborative ventures where all members are actively involved in daily operations.

Conversely, a manager-managed LLC allows members to appoint one or more managers, who may or may not be members themselves. This structure can be beneficial for larger LLCs or for members who prefer to be passive investors rather than engage in day-to-day management. Each structure impacts the dynamics of business operations and decision-making processes, influencing everything from daily activities to strategic direction.

Steps to Set Up an LLC

Setting up an LLC, while simpler than forming a corporation, involves several key steps that require careful attention. Initially, you must choose a unique name for your LLC that complies with state regulations. This process typically involves a name search to ensure availability. Following this, filing the Articles of Organization with your state's Secretary of State is essential. This foundational document outlines basic information about your LLC, including the name, principal office address, and the names of the members, and it officially marks the creation of your LLC.

Depending on your state, you may also be required to publish a notice of intent to form an LLC in a local newspaper. This step varies by state but is often a necessary part of the formation process.

Reflecting on older business practices that aimed to keep the public informed, each of these steps, though straightforward, is crucial in laying the groundwork for your business. They set the stage for a detailed exploration of how to navigate these processes efficiently in the upcoming chapters.

Evaluating State-Specific LLC Rules and Requirements

When forming an LLC, one critical aspect that often catches new entrepreneurs off guard is the variability of rules and requirements across states. Each state in the U.S. has the authority to establish its own regulations governing the formation, operation, and dissolution of LLCs. This variability can significantly affect everything from the paperwork you need to file to the fees you'll pay and even the tax implications of your business decisions. Navigating this landscape requires a proactive approach to gathering and interpreting state-specific information.

To begin, identify the state in which you intend to register your LLC, typically the state where your business will primarily operate. Each state has a Secretary of State office or an equivalent department responsible for business registrations. These offices are treasure troves of information, providing details about the necessary forms, fees, and legal requirements specific to your state. Many states have also transitioned to online services, offering resources such as downloadable forms, filing instructions, and even online registration systems that simplify the LLC setup process.

However, simply accessing this information isn't enough; you must also interpret it correctly. State-specific nuances in LLC regulations can include differences in annual fees, variations in privacy laws affecting what information you must publicly disclose, and distinct operational rules that could dictate how you structure your LLC management. For example, some states require an annual report to update the state on your LLC's members and business activities, while others do not. Misinterpreting these rules can lead to non-compliance, resulting in fines, legal disputes, or even the dissolution of your business entity by the state.

The importance of adhering to state regulations cannot be overstated. Compliance ensures that your LLC remains in good standing and is legally recognized as an independent entity separate from its owners. This separation is essential for maintaining the limited liability protection that likely motivated your choice of an LLC structure in the first place. Common compliance issues often arise from failing to properly update the state on changes within the company, such as shifts in membership or business address, or lapses in renewing necessary permits and licenses. Staying proactive in meeting these requirements can save you from future headaches and potential legal challenges.

Additionally, understanding how state-specific rules impact taxes and legal obligations underscores the importance of local regulations. For instance, the way your LLC is taxed can vary dramatically depending on the state.

While the federal government allows LLCs to choose between being taxed as a partnership or a corporation, individual states may impose additional tax obligations or offer incentives. For example, states like

Wyoming provide significant tax advantages that can be beneficial for LLCs, potentially influencing your decision on where to establish your business. Conversely, states like California impose a franchise tax on all LLCs, which is a crucial factor to consider during the financial planning phase of your business setup.

Given the complexity and significance of state-specific regulations, accessing reliable resources is indispensable. Start with official state websites, which typically serve as the most authoritative sources for regulatory and procedural information. Legal aid organizations can also offer guidance and sometimes free consultations to help you navigate state laws. Websites like the U.S. Small Business Administration (SBA) provide tools and detailed guides that can be extremely helpful. Additionally, consider investing in consultation services with a local attorney who specializes in business law. Their expertise can provide insights into current laws, recent changes, and relevant local legal precedents that could impact your business.

Navigating the maze of state-specific regulations may seem daunting, but with the right resources and a meticulous approach, you can establish and operate your LLC with confidence, ensuring compliance while maximizing state-specific benefits and protections.

The Importance of a Business Plan in LLC Formation

Creating a business plan is not just a formality; it's a vital roadmap that guides your LLC from concept to fully operational entity. Think of it as laying down tracks for a train; without these tracks, the train would aimlessly wander without direction. A well-structured business plan consolidates your vision, strategies, and goals into a coherent framework that persuades investors and lenders of your seriousness while providing a blueprint for managing your business's growth and development.

Structuring a Business Plan

A robust business plan covers all the critical aspects of your business. The executive summary, although the first section, is best written last. It should provide a snapshot of your business and its potential, capturing the essence of what your business is about, the market opportunity, your approach to capitalizing on that opportunity, and the specifics of your financial projections. This summary is crucial, as it is often the only section read by potential investors; therefore, it needs to be compelling and concise.

The market analysis section should build upon the market insights you've already gathered. Here, detail your understanding of the industry, market trends, target demographics, and the competitive landscape. This section should articulate who your customers are and how you plan to attract them away from competitors.

The organizational structure section outlines your business's operational framework. It details who is managing what, their roles, and their areas of expertise. Additionally, this part should explain the legal structure of your LLC and clarify how decisions are made within the company. This structure is essential for defining the chain of command and ensuring accountability across various functions.

Product or Service Line

Next, provide an in-depth description of your product or service line. What are you selling? Highlight the key features and benefits of your offerings, and explain how they meet the needs identified in your market analysis. This section should be detailed enough to make it clear what customers can expect from your products or services, showcasing how they fulfill specific demands or solve particular problems.

Financial Projections

The financial projections section translates all aspects of your business plan into numbers. Project your revenues, expenses, and profitability over a reasonable time frame. This part should not only demonstrate the potential for profitability but also include a break-even analysis, cash flow projections, and various scenarios illustrating how your business can handle potential setbacks. Clear and realistic financial projections will instill confidence in potential investors and stakeholders.

Role in Securing Financing

When it comes to securing financing, your business plan serves as your best advocate. Banks and investors need assurance that your business idea is viable and that you have a clear strategy for making it profitable. They want to understand the risks involved and see that you have strategies in place to mitigate these risks. Your financial projections should be realistic and data-driven, clearly demonstrating your understanding of the financial dynamics of your business. Detailed market analysis supports this by showing a deep understanding of your market and competition, which helps convince financiers that you are equipped to navigate industry challenges.

Tool for Strategic Planning and Management

Beyond securing funds, your business plan is an indispensable tool for strategic planning and management. It acts as a roadmap, guiding your decision-making process as your business evolves. It should be a living document, one that adapts as your LLC grows. Regularly revisiting and revising your business plan in response to market changes, financial realities, and operational results is crucial. This practice helps you stay on track toward your goals and enables informed decisions that align with your long-term objectives.

Adapting the Plan for Different Audiences

Lastly, remember that one size does not fit all when it comes to presenting your business plan. The emphasis of your plan may shift depending on who is reading it. For investors, focus on growth potential and return on investment. For banks, stability and repayment ability might be more critical. For business partners, operational capabilities and market advantages could be of greater interest. Tailoring your business plan according to your audience's interests can make your case more persuasive and demonstrate your adaptability and strategic thinking.

A well-crafted business plan not only aids in securing necessary funding but also serves as a critical tool for effectively managing your business. It provides a detailed roadmap for your LLC's operations, facilitates strategic oversight, and prepares your business to adapt to the needs and interests of various stakeholders. By investing time and effort into developing a comprehensive business plan, you lay a strong foundation for the sustainable growth and success of your LLC.

Setting Up Your Business Goals and Vision

The foundation of a successful LLC begins not only with a solid business plan but also with clearly defined goals and a compelling vision. These elements act as guiding stars for your business, helping navigate the often-turbulent waters of entrepreneurship. By establishing specific, measurable, achievable, relevant, and time-bound (SMART) goals, you create a framework that propels your business forward and provides benchmarks for measuring progress.

SMART goals ensure that every objective you set is Specific, Measurable, Achievable, Relevant, and Time-bound. For instance, instead of a vague goal like "increase sales," a SMART goal would be "increase sales by 20% within the next 12 months." This goal is specific, measurable, and time-bound, with a clear target that is directly relevant to the broader objectives of your LLC. Setting such goals transforms abstract aspirations into concrete targets, making the path to success clear and actionable.

The significance of a strong vision statement cannot be overstated. This concise declaration of your business's long-term intentions serves as a constant reminder of what you are striving to achieve. It forms the core from which all business strategies should emanate, inspiring and aligning your team and stakeholders toward your objectives. For example, a vision statement like "To empower small businesses through innovative financial solutions" clearly communicates the company's long-term goal and its commitment to a specific market segment and value proposition.

Aligning your business goals with market needs is another critical aspect of strategic planning. This alignment ensures that your business remains relevant and competitive in a changing market. It involves staying attuned to customer feedback, market trends, and shifts in the industry landscape, using this information to fine-tune your strategies. For example, if customer feedback indicates a growing demand for a particular service, you might set a goal to expand that service line, ensuring your offerings continue to meet market needs effectively.

Regularly monitoring and revising your goals is just as crucial as setting them. The business world is dynamic, with constant changes in market conditions, consumer behavior, and technology. By reviewing your goals regularly, you can ensure they remain aligned with your business's direction and responsive to emerging challenges and opportunities.

To ensure your goals remain aligned with both your business vision and the current market environment, implement strategies such as quarterly reviews of your business plan and objectives. Be prepared to make adjustments as necessary, which may involve redefining targets, extending timelines, or revising your business's strategic direction to better align with emerging opportunities or challenges.

Adopting a flexible, responsive approach to goal management can significantly enhance your business's agility and resilience, empowering it to thrive in competitive and ever-changing markets. This active engagement with your goals keeps your business strategies effective and ensures that your entire organization remains aligned and focused on common objectives, driving collective efforts toward achieving significant milestones.

By embedding these practices into the fabric of your business operations, you establish a robust foundation for sustained growth and success. Your vision transcends mere words; it becomes a palpable influence propelling your business forward. Your goals evolve from mere aspirations into tangible outcomes, charting the course for your business's future. As you continue to refine these objectives, remember that the clarity of your vision and the precision of your goals will often dictate the heights your business can reach.

CHAPTER

TWO

The Formation Process

Imagine the moment you decide to turn your business idea into reality. It's exhilarating, isn't it? However, as you transition from ideation to execution, the first critical step you confront is naming your LLC. While this may seem like a simple task, it is laden with legal intricacies, strategic branding decisions, and vital procedural steps that can significantly influence your business's trajectory. In this section, you will learn not just how to select a name, but how to craft an identity that aligns with your business ethos, adheres to legal standards, and captivates your target market.

Naming Your LLC: A Step-by-Step Guide

Understanding Naming Guidelines

Every state in the U.S. has its own set of rules governing the naming of new business entities. A common requirement is that your LLC's name must be distinguishable from the names of existing businesses already registered in the state. This helps avoid confusion and protects established brands. Additionally, your business name must include an indicator of your business type, such as "LLC," "L.L.C.," or "Limited

Liability Company." This not only complies with state laws but also signals to customers and partners the legal structure of your business, influencing their perceptions of credibility and trustworthiness.

However, the guidelines do not stop there. Most states prohibit the use of certain words that could mislead the public about the nature of your business. For instance, terms like "Bank," "Attorney," or "University" may require additional licenses and approvals to use. Understanding these restrictions is crucial to avoid potential legal pitfalls as you establish your brand.

To navigate these rules effectively, begin by visiting your state's Secretary of State website, where you can access detailed resources on naming conventions. Understanding these guidelines is crucial not only for legal compliance but also to prevent costly rebranding exercises if your chosen name doesn't meet regulatory standards.

Conducting a Name Search

Once you're familiar with the naming guidelines, the next step is to ensure that your chosen name isn't already taken. This involves performing a name search through your state's business registry, typically available online via the Secretary of State's website. But don't stop there—also check for online domain availability. In today's digital world, having a matching domain name can significantly enhance your online presence and marketing efforts. Tools like WHOIS domain lookup can help you determine if your desired website domain is available or already in use. This dual approach ensures that your chosen name is both legally compliant and uniquely yours in the digital landscape.

Evaluating Brand Impact

Choosing the right name is a powerful branding opportunity. Your LLC's name is often the first interaction potential customers have with your business—it sets the tone and expectations. Therefore, it should resonate with your target audience and reflect your business's values and mission. Consider the emotions and impressions you want the name to evoke. Does it convey reliability, innovation, or perhaps eco-friendliness? Engage in brainstorming sessions, consider your audience's language and culture, and test potential names with friends, family, or target audience samples to gauge impact. Remember, a well-chosen name can be a significant asset, enhancing your marketing efforts and building public trust.

Registering the Name

After settling on a name and ensuring it meets all legal criteria and branding objectives, the final step is to register it with your state. This typically involves filing a Name Reservation form with your state's Secretary of State office, either online or by mail, accompanied by a nominal fee. While this reservation doesn't yet make your business operational, it secures your chosen name for a limited period—usually 60 to 120 days—giving you time to file your Articles of Organization, which we will explore in the next sections. Ensure you gather all necessary information and complete all sections of the form accurately to avoid delays. Once submitted, you'll receive confirmation, and your business name will be officially reserved. This marks a significant milestone in your business setup process, bringing you one step closer to launching your vision into the world.

As you embark on this naming adventure, remember that each decision you make sets the stage for your brand's narrative and public perception. A thoughtful, strategic approach to naming your LLC can pave the way for a strong brand identity and market recognition.

Designing and Filing Your Articles of Organization

When you're ready to formalize your business as an LLC, the Articles of Organization serve as the official birth certificate of your venture, outlining its existence and structure to the state. While this document may seem straightforward, it contains critical elements that must be carefully crafted to ensure compliance and legitimacy for your business.

Key Components of the Articles of Organization

Business Name: Start by including your LLC's name, which should adhere to the naming conventions and restrictions of your state, as previously secured during your name reservation process.

Principal Address: Provide the principal address of your business, which is the primary location where your business activities will be conducted. This address is essential not only for legal notices but also for tax purposes and public records.

Member Information: This section details the members (owners) of the LLC and their respective ownership percentages. Transparency in ownership is crucial for both legal and operational purposes, as it defines who has authority and responsibility within the company.

Registered Agent Details: Include information about the registered agent, who acts as your LLC's official point of contact for legal correspondence. Choosing a reliable and consistently available agent ensures that you never miss important legal notices, which could have significant implications for your business.

Filing the Articles of Organization

Filing the Articles of Organization involves understanding your state's submission process. Most states offer the convenience of online filing, which provides speed and real-time updates. Alternatively, you can file by mail, though this option may lead to longer processing times. Each method incurs a filing fee, which varies from state to state, so be sure to budget for this cost as part of your initial expenses. Processing times can also vary, generally ranging from a few days to several weeks. During this waiting period, keep a close eye on the status of your filing through the state's business filing agency website or direct contact.

Common Pitfalls to Avoid

A common pitfall in filing Articles of Organization is overlooking the specificity and accuracy required in the document. Simple mistakes—such as misspellings, incorrect addresses, or incomplete member information—can cause delays or rejections of your filing. To avoid these issues, double-check every piece of information you enter. Utilize professional legal forms or services if necessary to ensure that all required details are appropriately documented and formatted.

Remember, this document not only establishes your business but also sets the legal framework within which it operates, so accuracy is paramount.

After Filing

Once your Articles of Organization have been successfully filed and approved, you will receive an official confirmation, typically in the form of a stamped copy of the Articles from the state. This confirmation serves as proof of your LLC status and should be kept securely, as it may be required for various legal and operational purposes in the future.

Business Records and Compliance:

Once your LLC is confirmed, it's important to be aware of any state-specific requirements. Some states mandate publishing the formation of a new LLC in a local newspaper to ensure public transparency. Others may require immediate registration for state taxes or obtaining an Employer Identification Number (EIN). Staying informed and addressing these requirements promptly keeps your LLC in good standing and avoids legal or financial penalties.

Diligently handling the design and filing of your Articles of Organization not only ensures legal compliance but also builds a strong administrative foundation for your business. This attention to detail early on sets the stage for efficient management as your business grows and evolves. The more thorough you are during the foundational phase, the smoother operations will be when future challenges arise.

Selecting a Registered Agent: A Key Decision

A registered agent plays a pivotal role in your LLC's compliance and operations. They receive important legal and tax documents on behalf of your LLC, such as service of process, government correspondence, and compliance notifications. In essence, your registered agent acts as the public face of your LLC for legal matters, ensuring you receive critical information that could impact your business's legal standing.

You have two options: appointing an individual (yourself or an associate) or hiring a professional registered agent service. Choosing someone you know might save costs, but it requires consistent availability during business hours to handle legal documents. If this is not feasible, missing important notices could lead to penalties or legal action.

Alternatively, professional registered agent services provide several advantages. They ensure timely handling of legal documents, maintain privacy by keeping your business address off public records, and assist with multi-state compliance if your LLC operates across state lines. Though this comes at a cost, the peace of mind and professionalism often justify the investment.

The Convenience of Professional Registered Agents

Professional registered agent services offer a significant advantage by allowing you to focus on running your business instead of handling administrative tasks. When selecting an agent, whether an individual or a service, several factors should guide your decision.

First, reliability is crucial. The agent must handle and forward legal documents promptly. Availability is also essential, as the agent must be present at the registered office during all standard business hours—a legal requirement to ensure your business can be reached by legal and government entities. Additionally, the agent should be knowledgeable about state legal requirements, especially if your LLC operates in multiple states. This expertise will help maintain compliance with varying laws and filing deadlines across jurisdictions.

Changing Your Registered Agent

If you need to change your registered agent, the process is generally straightforward. You might decide to switch to a professional service after initially appointing yourself, or you could find a service that offers better support or value. Changing agents involves filing a change of agent form with the state where your LLC is registered, along with a small filing fee. It's essential to ensure no gap in service during the transition. Appoint your new agent before discharging the current one, and notify all relevant parties promptly to avoid any misdirected legal documents. Proper management of this transition ensures continuity and safeguards your business's legal standing.

The Importance of Choosing the Right Agent

Selecting a registered agent is a decision that impacts the smooth operation and compliance of your LLC. Missing or mishandling legal documents can have far-reaching consequences, so it's important to make an informed choice that ensures your business stays protected.

Drafting Your LLC Operating Agreement

Another crucial step in forming an LLC is drafting the Operating Agreement. While the Articles of Organization legally register your business with the state, the Operating Agreement acts as an internal guide that governs your LLC's management, financial structure, and operational processes. This document defines the roles and responsibilities of members, the allocation of profits and losses, and procedures for dispute resolution or changes in membership.

Even in states where an Operating Agreement is not legally required, it's still highly beneficial. Without one, your LLC will be governed by the state's default rules, which may not suit your business's specific needs. By creating a tailored Operating Agreement, you establish a clear framework that can prevent conflicts and ensure your LLC runs smoothly according to the members' preferences, not just default state laws. In short, drafting a comprehensive Operating Agreement is not only recommended but a strategic necessity for long-term success.

Key Components to Include in Your Operating Agreement

A well-drafted Operating Agreement should address several core components to ensure clarity in your LLC's operations and governance.

Membership Interests: Clearly outline the ownership percentages of each member, their capital contributions, and how profits and losses will be distributed. This prevents financial misunderstandings and sets clear expectations for all members.

Management Duties: Specify whether your LLC will be member-managed or manager-managed. In a member-managed LLC, all members share decision-making responsibilities, whereas in a manager-managed LLC, certain individuals or external managers handle daily operations. Clearly define the powers and duties of the managers to establish guidelines for what they can or cannot do without member approval.

Voting Rights: Establish how decisions will be made. This includes defining a quorum for voting purposes and how votes will be counted. Typically, voting is proportionate to ownership, but this can be customized to fit your LLC's specific needs. This section should also cover the process for adding or removing members, including how new members are admitted and how exits are handled financially and operationally.

Dispute Resolution: Outline the procedures for resolving disputes among members. This can help prevent conflicts from escalating and ensures that disagreements are managed in a structured manner.

Procedures for Membership Changes: Include provisions for how to handle the departure of a member, whether through voluntary exit, death, or other circumstances. Address how their interests will be redistributed or bought out, ensuring a smooth transition.

These buy-sell provisions ensure that if a member decides to sell their interest, passes away, or becomes incapacitated, the LLC can continue operating smoothly without disruption. By addressing these potential scenarios in advance, you protect the business from unnecessary legal or financial complications and ensure a seamless transition for the remaining members.

Legal Compliance and Updates

Your Operating Agreement must adhere to state laws. While many states provide flexibility in what can be included in an Operating Agreement, some impose specific requirements or restrictions. To ensure compliance, always review your state's LLC laws, particularly regarding member rights, profit distribution, and management structures. It's also advisable to have a legal professional review the document to ensure it doesn't include any provisions that are illegal or unenforceable.

Additionally, your Operating Agreement should evolve as your business grows. Changes in management, ownership percentages, or even state laws may require updates to the agreement. It's essential to establish a protocol for amendments within the document itself. This protocol should outline how changes are proposed, voted on, and ratified, ensuring all members remain aligned and that the document stays relevant and compliant.

A well-thought-out Operating Agreement lays the foundation for a healthy LLC. By addressing all critical components and customizing the document to meet your business's unique needs, you create a framework that helps mitigate conflicts and ensures smooth operations. While drafting the agreement requires effort, the clarity and organization it brings are invaluable for your business's long-term success.

Obtaining Licenses and Permits

Securing the appropriate licenses and permits is a crucial, though sometimes overwhelming, step in forming an LLC. These permits ensure your business operates legally and within regulatory boundaries. Whether it's a local food safety permit for a restaurant or a federal environmental permit for a construction project, knowing what permits your LLC needs is vital.

Start by researching local, state, and federal government websites that outline the necessary permits for your business type and location. For additional guidance, reaching out to local chambers of commerce or business advocacy groups can provide specific insights relevant to your industry and area.

Different businesses have distinct requirements. For example, a retail store may need a city business license, a state sales tax permit, and potentially a federal consumer product safety certificate. In contrast, a manufacturing business may require environmental permits and certifications for heavy machinery. Creating a comprehensive list of regulatory requirements across all levels ensures you remain compliant, avoid legal issues, and streamline your business operations to align with government standards from the start.

The process of applying for permits and licenses typically involves completing detailed application forms, submitting necessary documentation (such as proof of business address, tax ID number, or specific qualifications), and paying applicable fees. It is advisable to approach this process with meticulous attention to detail, as misinformation or missing documents can lead to delays or denials that may hinder your business's opening or expansion plans. Many jurisdictions now offer online application portals, which can expedite the process and provide real-time updates on your application status. However, if you need to interact with multiple departments or navigate complex requirements, consider hiring a professional licenser or legal expert specializing in business compliance. Their expertise can save you time and mitigate compliance risks.

Understanding the costs associated with obtaining and renewing licenses and permits is also critical. These costs can vary widely based on the type of license, the location of your business, and the specific regulatory requirements involved. Some permits may have a one-time fee, while others require annual renewals. Budgeting for these costs should be an integral part of your financial planning to ensure operational liquidity and compliance. Additionally, maintaining a calendar of renewal deadlines is essential. Many businesses falter by overlooking a critical permit renewal, leading to suspended operations or hefty fines.

For businesses operating in physical locations or requiring significant modifications to existing properties, understanding and complying with zoning and land use laws is crucial. Zoning laws dictate what types of business activities can occur in certain areas, affecting everything from opening a new office to expanding a factory. Before signing a lease or purchasing property, confirm that the zoning regulations align with your intended use. If your business needs require a change in existing zoning, you will need to apply for a variance or a conditional use permit, which can be a complex process involving public hearings and detailed documentation.

Though these steps may seem complex, they are foundational for establishing a compliant and stable business operation. As you navigate the intricacies of licenses and permits, remember that this groundwork is not just about meeting legal requirements; it is about laying a robust framework for your business to thrive within the regulated parameters of your industry and region.

In conclusion, Chapter 2 of The Formation Process equips you with the knowledge and tools necessary to navigate the critical early stages of establishing your LLC—from selecting a resonant and compliant business name to understanding the intricate web of licenses and permits required for your specific operations. These foundational elements not only ensure the legality of your LLC but also support its potential for long-term success and stability. As we move forward, the next chapter will explore the financial aspects of setting up your LLC, guiding you through effective financial management practices that will foster your business's growth and sustainability.

CHAPTER
THREE

Financial Foundations

Imagine standing at the crossroads of an enchanting entrepreneurial landscape, where paths diverge toward various avenues of financing. Each path presents its unique set of challenges and rewards, whispering promises of growth and innovation. As you prepare to make decisions that will profoundly impact the financial health and structure of your LLC, understanding the nuances of initial funding becomes not just beneficial but essential. This chapter is dedicated to unraveling the complexities of financing your business venture, guiding you through the intricacies of bootstrapping versus investor funding, and laying out strategic approaches to managing your financial relationships.

Initial Funding: Bootstrapping vs. Seeking Investors

Pros and Cons of Bootstrapping

Bootstrapping—funding your business through personal savings and operational revenues—holds a certain allure for many entrepreneurs. This method champions self-reliance and minimizes debt, allowing you to maintain full control over your business decisions without the influence of external stakeholders. Picture yourself at the helm of your enterprise, steering your business with unbridled autonomy, each decision undiluted by investor interests or preferences.

However, this freedom comes with its caveats. Limited funds can lead to slower growth and may restrict your ability to capitalize on market opportunities quickly. The scale and scope of your project might be constrained by the depth of your financial reservoir, potentially resulting in a slower pace of business development and expansion.

Exploring Investor Funding Options

In contrast, seeking investor funding opens a spectrum of possibilities through financial avenues like angel investors, venture capital, and crowdfunding platforms. Each of these options unlocks different scales of funding, resources, and networking opportunities.

Angel investors, often affluent individuals looking to support startups, provide not only capital but also valuable mentorship and access to industry networks. Venture capitalists offer substantial sums that can catapult your business to new heights, though this often comes at the cost of partial ownership and a say in business decisions. Crowdfunding, the collective effort of individuals to fund a business via platforms like Kickstarter, presents a way to raise capital directly from future customers and supporters, enhancing market validation before a full-scale product launch.

Navigating Investor Dynamics

Navigating these waters requires a keen understanding of what each type of investor seeks in a potential investment. Angel investors often prioritize a compelling vision or a strong personal connection with the entrepreneur. In contrast, venture capitalists typically focus on potential returns on investment, scalability, and market size. Success in crowdfunding usually hinges on the ability to market a product or idea that resonates with a broad audience and presents an appealing or innovative solution to existing problems.

Preparing to Pitch to Investors

Crafting a compelling pitch is an art form that balances data, storytelling, and strategic foresight. Your pitch to potential investors should encapsulate not only the essence of your business but also articulate its potential for growth, competitive advantages, and a clear path to profitability. Essential elements include an overview of the market size, detailed customer segmentation, your business model, and financial projections that highlight potential returns.

This is your moment to shine—to convey passion, depth of knowledge, and the viability of your business. Investors are looking for confidence not only in the business but in the entrepreneur leading the charge. They invest in your vision and your ability to execute that vision.

Managing Investor Relationships

Once investors are on board, managing those relationships becomes crucial to ongoing business success. Regular, transparent communication is key. Update your investors on both successes and setbacks. This approach fosters trust and enables your investors to offer support or advice when needed. Setting clear expectations from the outset about the frequency and type of updates, such as quarterly financial reports or monthly progress emails, can help manage investor expectations and keep them engaged in your business journey.

Furthermore, understanding investor expectations and aligning them with your business goals can mitigate potential conflicts and ensure a harmonious relationship. Be proactive in discussions about business strategies and growth opportunities. Engaging investors in such conversations not only leverages their experience and insights but also reinforces their commitment to your success.

As you navigate the initial stages of funding your LLC, remember that each choice you make in financing your business can significantly influence its structure, culture, and operational dynamics. Whether you choose to bootstrap your business, embrace investor funding, or combine various financing approaches, understanding the benefits and challenges of each will be crucial in laying a robust financial foundation for your business.

Opening a Business Bank Account

When you decide to open a business bank account, you're setting a cornerstone for your LLC's financial management and operational efficiency. Choosing the right bank and the appropriate account type can significantly influence your day-to-day business operations and long-term financial strategy.

When selecting a bank, start by considering the fees associated with the account. Some banks offer free business checking accounts, but be mindful of potential hidden fees for transactions, wire transfers, or minimum balance requirements. Additionally, the services provided by the bank are paramount. Look for services that align with your business needs, such as online banking, mobile deposits, or specialized loan services. These features can offer convenience and flexibility, saving you time and effort in managing your business finances.

Choosing the Right Bank

The accessibility of the bank's physical locations and the efficacy of their online banking services are crucial factors to consider. If your business requires regular cash deposits or face-to-face consultations, a bank with nearby branches is beneficial. Conversely, if you prefer handling most of your transactions online, ensure the bank offers a robust and secure online platform. Additionally, some banks provide tailored services for LLCs and might even offer advisory services to help you navigate the early stages of your business setup. These banks can become partners in your entrepreneurial journey, offering insights and resources that go beyond mere financial transactions.

The Account Opening Process

The process of opening a business bank account typically begins with gathering the necessary documentation. The most fundamental document you need is your Employer Identification Number (EIN), sometimes referred to as your business tax ID number. This number is essential not just for banking but also for various business operations, including tax filings and employee payroll. Most banks will also request your LLC's Articles of Organization to verify the legal existence of your business. If multiple members in your LLC will have access to the account, you might also need to provide a resolution identifying authorized signers. This preparation ensures that all transactions are legitimate and that all members with access are accounted for legally and transparently.

Once you've gathered the necessary documentation, the next step involves visiting the bank to open the account, though some banks may offer options to complete this process online. During the account opening process, you'll decide on the type of account that best suits your business needs. Most businesses start with a checking account for handling day-to-day transactions, but consider whether you might also need a savings account to earn interest on your profits or a credit account to help finance larger expenses. Discuss these options with your banking representative to ensure you choose the right accounts for your business's financial health and growth.

Separating Personal and Business Finances

One of the fundamental rules in managing an LLC is to keep personal and business finances separate. This separation simplifies accounting processes, enhances transparency, and is crucial for accurate tax reporting. It helps clearly delineate personal and business expenses, which can be critical in the event of an audit. Furthermore, it reinforces the legal distinction between you as an individual and your business, which is essential for maintaining your limited liability protection. This separation starts with having dedicated business banking accounts and extends to all areas of financial management, including credit card transactions and loan applications.

Understanding and Managing Business Credit

Understanding and managing business credit is vital for your LLC's financial future. Business credit, similar to personal credit, is a record of your business's financial responsibility that lenders use to evaluate creditworthiness for loans, credit lines, and payment terms with suppliers. Building a strong business credit score begins with basic steps, such as ensuring your business is listed with credit reporting agencies and maintaining good credit by paying creditors on time.

Additionally, consider opening a business credit card, which, when used responsibly, can help you build your credit score while providing flexibility in managing cash flow. Using business credit wisely involves understanding the terms of credit, interest rates, and the potential impact on your business's financial health.

Regularly reviewing your credit agreements and monitoring your business credit score is essential to ensure it accurately reflects your financial practices and remains a strong asset for your business. Responsible management of business credit not only facilitates easier access to financing when needed but also contributes to the overall financial stability and credibility of your LLC.

Understanding LLC Tax Classifications

Navigating the tax landscape of an LLC can feel like decoding a complex puzzle, where each piece represents a different tax implication that could significantly impact your business's financial health.

LLCs stand out due to their flexibility in tax classification, offering several options that cater to various business sizes, structures, and goals.

By default, an LLC is treated as a disregarded entity if it has one member or as a partnership if it has two or more members. However, it can also elect to be treated as an S corporation. Understanding these classifications and their implications helps in making informed decisions that align with your business strategy and financial planning.

A disregarded entity is so named because the IRS disregards the separate entity for tax purposes, meaning the business itself isn't taxed directly. Instead, all profits and losses are passed through to the owner's personal tax returns. This setup simplifies the tax filing process but also means that your business income is subject to self-employment taxes, which cover Social Security and Medicare. For single-member LLCs, this classification avoids the double taxation faced by traditional corporations but may result in potentially higher personal taxes, depending on your income level.

In contrast, if your LLC has more than one member, it will default to a partnership for tax purposes. Like the disregarded entity, a partnership itself is not taxed. Instead, income is passed through to the members, who then report it on their personal tax returns. This setup fosters flexibility in how profits and losses are distributed among members, according to the stipulations laid out in the LLC operating agreement.

It's crucial to ensure that the operating agreement clearly defines these terms to avoid confusion and ensure equitable tax reporting among members.

S Corporation Election

Alternatively, your LLC can elect to be treated as an S corporation by filing IRS Form 2553. This option offers potential tax savings associated with self-employment taxes. With an S corporation, only salaries paid to employees (including owner-operators) are subject to employment taxes. Any additional profits are distributed as dividends, which are taxed at a potentially lower rate and are not subject to self-employment taxes. This can be particularly advantageous for higher-earning LLCs, where savings on self-employment taxes can be significant. However, it's important to note that the S corporation structure imposes stricter operational requirements, including salary requirements for owners and limits on the number and type of shareholders.

If considering a shift from the default classification, the process involves submitting IRS Form 8832 for C corporation treatment or Form 2553 for S corporation treatment. This decision should not be taken lightly, as it can have long-lasting implications on your financial operations and tax obligations. The choice to change your tax classification might be driven by various factors, including changes in business size, the introduction of new members, or shifts in your financial strategy. Consulting with a tax advisor is advisable to fully understand the implications of each option and to ensure the chosen classification aligns with both your current circumstances and future business goals.

Practical Implications of Tax Classifications

To illustrate the practical implications of these tax classifications, consider a few scenarios:

Single-Member LLC: Imagine a single-member LLC consulting business that has opted to be treated as a disregarded entity. As the owner reports all business income on their personal tax returns, they find themselves paying significant amounts in self-employment taxes as their business grows. In response, they elect to be treated as an S corporation. By doing so, they can pay themselves a reasonable salary

subject to employment taxes, with the remainder taken as a distribution, potentially lowering their overall tax liability.

Multi-Member LLC: Now, consider a multi-member LLC that operates as a partnership. The members enjoy the flexibility of allocating profits according to their operating agreement, which may not necessarily align with their ownership percentages. This flexibility allows them to strategically manage financial contributions and tax implications based on each member's circumstances.

Each of these scenarios underscores the importance of understanding the tax classifications available to LLCs and choosing the one that best suits your business's financial needs and goals. As you navigate these decisions, remember that the clarity of your operational agreements and the strategic management of your tax obligations are pivotal in optimizing your business's financial health.

Essential Bookkeeping Practices for New LLCs

Setting up an effective bookkeeping system from the outset is akin to laying a robust foundation for a building—it supports every subsequent layer of your business operations and financial management. Whether you opt for a manual system or a software-based solution, the key is to ensure that the system is scalable, accessible, and tailored to meet the specific needs of your LLC.

Starting with a manual system might seem cost-effective and straightforward, involving physical ledgers or simple spreadsheets. However, as your business grows, the limitations of a manual system can quickly become apparent, leading to increased time spent on bookkeeping tasks and a higher potential for human error. In contrast, a software-based bookkeeping system may require an initial investment in both money and time to learn the software, but it can dramatically increase efficiency. Modern bookkeeping software offers features such as automatic data entry, integration with bank accounts and payment systems, comprehensive financial reporting, and even remote access, which can be invaluable as your business scales.

Setting Up Your Bookkeeping System

The process of establishing your bookkeeping system should start with a clear understanding of your business's financial transactions and requirements. Identify the types of transactions your business engages in regularly, such as sales, purchases, payroll, and investments. This identification will guide you in setting up appropriate accounts within your bookkeeping system, ensuring that all types of transactions are accurately categorized and recorded.

If you choose to use bookkeeping software, take advantage of customization options to tailor the system to your business's needs. This might involve setting up custom categories for expenses or integrating the software with other systems you use, such as point-of-sale systems or e-commerce platforms. Additionally, consider the security features of the system, especially if you opt for cloud-based software, to protect sensitive financial data from unauthorized access or data breaches.

Recording Transactions Accurately

The importance of accurately recording every financial transaction cannot be overstated. Each sale, expense, and investment must be recorded with precision, as these records form the basis of your financial statements and tax returns. Accurate record-keeping not only ensures compliance with accounting standards and tax laws but also provides you with a clear picture of your business's financial health, informing your decision-making process.

To achieve accuracy, develop a routine for recording transactions as soon as they occur. This might involve daily entries into your bookkeeping system or scheduled weekly updates to catch up on any transactions recorded elsewhere, such as in sales logs or on receipts.

Training for you or your staff on how to use your chosen bookkeeping system effectively is crucial. Misunderstandings or mistakes in entering data can lead to inaccurate financial reports that could misinform your business decisions or even lead to legal complications. Consider investing in training sessions provided by software vendors or hiring a professional bookkeeper in the initial stages to set up your system and train your team. This upfront investment can save considerable time and money by preventing errors and ensuring that your financial recording processes are efficient and compliant with relevant standards.

Understanding Financial Statements

For many new LLC owners, financial statements can seem daunting, filled with arrays of numbers and accounting jargon. However, developing an understanding of these documents is crucial, as they provide invaluable insights into your business's financial status and trajectories. The three primary financial statements you should become familiar with are the balance sheet, income statement, and cash flow statement.

Balance Sheet: This document provides a snapshot of your business's financial standing at a specific point in time. It shows what your business owns (assets) and owes (liabilities), along with the equity held by the owners.

Income Statement: Also known as the profit and loss statement, this shows how much money your business made and spent over a period, offering a summary of operational efficiency and profitability.

Cash Flow Statement: This statement tracks the flow of cash in and out of your business, highlighting how well your company manages its cash to fund operations and growth.

To effectively utilize these financial statements, start by reviewing them regularly—at least quarterly. Look for trends, such as increasing expenses or fluctuations in revenue, which could indicate underlying issues or opportunities for growth. Use the insights gained from these statements to make informed decisions about budget adjustments, potential investments, or cost-cutting measures.

Regular Review and Reconciliation

Regular review and reconciliation of your financial records are essential practices that ensure the accuracy and reliability of your financial reporting. Reconciliation involves comparing your internal financial records against external records, such as bank statements, to verify that they match. This process helps you catch and correct discrepancies in your records, such as double entries, omitted transactions, or mathematical errors. Additionally, it provides an extra layer of security by helping you identify any potential fraudulent activity.

Set a regular schedule for reviewing and reconciling your financial records; for many businesses, a monthly review is sufficient. This routine should include checking all financial statements and ledgers to ensure they accurately reflect your business transactions, making adjustments as necessary to rectify discrepancies. Regular reviews not only help maintain accurate records but also provide ongoing insights into your business's financial health, allowing you to respond quickly to any issues that could impact your financial stability or growth opportunities.

Incorporating these practices into your routine not only streamlines your financial management but also reinforces the overall strategic management of your LLC. As you continue to build and refine your financial practices, these routines will become second nature, providing a steady foundation of accurate, reliable financial information that supports the growth and sustainability of your business.

Planning for Annual Taxes

Anticipating your annual tax obligations involves a thoughtful review of your business's financial performance throughout the year and an understanding of how different tax classifications impact your tax responsibilities. Start by examining your income streams, expenditures, and any potential taxable events. This comprehensive financial overview not only prepares you for accurate tax filings but also enhances your understanding of your business's financial health.

Maintaining meticulous records of all business transactions is essential, as these will form the basis of your tax calculations. Depending on your LLC's tax classification—whether treated as a disregarded entity, a partnership, or an S corporation—the method for computing taxes will vary. For instance, if your LLC is treated as a disregarded entity, your business income passes through to your personal tax returns, requiring you to account for this in your personal tax preparation.

Additionally, consider the timing of significant transactions, such as large purchases or sales, which may impact your tax liability. If possible, consult with a tax professional who can provide insights into effective tax planning strategies. This might include deferring income to the next tax year or accelerating expenses to offset income. Such strategies can help you manage your tax obligations more effectively, ensuring that you maximize your cash flow while remaining compliant with tax laws.

Making Quarterly Estimated Tax Payments

For many LLC owners, making quarterly estimated tax payments is a critical aspect of financial management. The IRS requires tax payments to be made throughout the year, not just at the end. Failure to comply can result in penalties and interest charges, which can create an unnecessary financial burden.

To manage this obligation, calculate your estimated tax liability based on your earnings for the year. This involves a good understanding of your current income and an accurate projection of your earnings in the coming quarters.

The process includes filling out IRS Form 1040-ES, which helps you estimate the amount of tax you owe for the year. Based on this form, you'll make payments in four equal installments due in April, June, September, and the following January. Setting calendar reminders for these due dates can be incredibly helpful in staying organized and on top of your obligations.

Additionally, consider setting aside a portion of your income regularly in a separate account earmarked for taxes. This practice ensures that funds are readily available when tax payments are due, avoiding the last-minute scramble to gather sufficient funds.

Taking Advantage of Deductions and Credits

Navigating the landscape of deductions and credits available to LLCs can significantly reduce your tax liability. Common deductions include business expenses such as office supplies, travel expenses, and salaries paid to employees. To maximize these deductions, it's essential to maintain detailed records of all business-related expenses throughout the year. This practice not only simplifies the tax filing process but also ensures that you can substantiate these deductions in case of an audit.

While credits can be more challenging to qualify for than deductions, they can also provide substantial reductions in your tax bill. Examples include credits for energy-efficient improvements to your business premises, hiring certain target groups, or engaging in research and development activities. Each credit comes with specific eligibility criteria, so it's important to review these carefully to determine if your LLC qualifies. Engaging a tax professional to identify and apply for these credits can be invaluable; they can offer guidance on documentation and the filing process, ensuring you take full advantage of these tax benefits.

Preparing for Year-End Tax Filing

As the year draws to a close, preparing for year-end tax filing becomes a top priority. Start by organizing your financial records, including receipts, bank statements, and invoices. This organization is crucial for an accurate and efficient filing process. Review your year-end financial statements to ensure they accurately reflect the true financial position of your business. These statements, along with your record of estimated tax payments and documentation of deductions and credits, will form the foundation of your tax filing.

Creating a checklist can streamline this process. Include tasks such as reconciling your books, finalizing payroll reports, and reviewing previous tax returns for any carryover items. Additionally, schedule a consultation with your tax advisor to discuss any changes in tax law that may affect your filing. This meeting is an opportunity to address any concerns about your tax situation and ensure that your returns are prepared accurately and in compliance with current laws.

By staying proactive in tax planning throughout the year, you can minimize last-minute surprises, optimize your financial outcomes, and ensure compliance with tax regulations. This preparation not only positions your LLC for financial stability but also provides peace of mind as you close out the year and plan for the future.

Conclusion

As we conclude this chapter on financial foundations, remember that the principles and practices outlined here are designed to fortify your understanding of financial management within your LLC. From making informed decisions about funding options to managing the intricacies of tax obligations and bookkeeping, each element plays a pivotal role in building a financially sound business.

As you move forward, keep these insights in mind to navigate the financial aspects of your business with confidence and clarity. In the next chapter, we will explore legal compliance and risk management, further expanding on the knowledge needed to secure and sustain your business in the competitive market landscape.

CHAPTER

FOUR

Legal Compliance
and Risk Management

Stepping into the realm of business ownership not only offers opportunities but also brings responsibilities—foremost among them is legal compliance. As you navigate the intricate weave of regulatory requirements and legal standards, understanding and adhering to compliance schedules becomes not just a protective measure but a strategic advantage. This chapter is designed to equip you with the knowledge and tools needed to establish a robust compliance framework for your LLC, ensuring that your business not only survives but thrives in the regulatory landscapes it operates within.

Annual Filings and Compliance Checklists

Understanding Annual Reporting Requirements

For many LLC owners, the annual report is a recurring notation on their corporate calendar. Yet, its significance extends far beyond a mere bureaucratic requirement. Most states mandate the submission of annual reports or statements for LLCs, which serve to update and confirm the details of your business as registered with the state. These reports typically include critical information such as current addresses, management structures, and registered agent details. The purpose? To ensure that the state has up-to-date information on your company, facilitating accurate communication and legal processes. This measure promotes transparency, supporting state oversight as well as public trust and corporate integrity.

The contents of these reports can vary significantly from state to state, highlighting the importance of familiarizing yourself with the specific requirements for each location where your LLC operates. Generally, you can expect to include details about any changes in your company's management or operational structure that have occurred over the past year, as well as updates regarding your principal place of business or registered agent. These filings typically incur a fee, which, although usually modest, should be accounted for in your annual budget. Failure to file these reports can lead to penalties, including fines or even the revocation of your business license.

Creating a Compliance Calendar

One of the most effective tools at your disposal is a compliance calendar—a strategic outline of all critical filing dates, legal obligations, and regulatory requirements your LLC must meet throughout the fiscal year. This proactive tool goes beyond mere organization; it ensures you never miss a deadline, thus avoiding unnecessary fines and legal complications that could arise from non-compliance.

Begin by marking out the due dates for your annual reports, tax filings, and any other state-specific filings that recur annually. Additionally, include quarterly or monthly obligations such as sales tax submissions or federal tax estimates. A well-maintained compliance calendar not only helps you stay organized but also reinforces a culture of accountability within your business, empowering you to focus on growth rather than getting bogged down by missed deadlines.

Integrating Your Compliance Calendar

For enhanced efficacy, integrate your compliance calendar with your digital or physical office calendars. Set reminders a few weeks in advance of each deadline to allow ample time for preparation and review. This integration ensures that compliance tasks are perceived as part of your regular business operations, rather than as an afterthought. The peace of mind that comes from knowing you are on top of every legal requirement allows you to focus more on growth and less on administrative concerns.

State-Specific Variations

The United States is a patchwork of regulatory environments, with each state establishing its own rules for business operations. Understanding these variations is crucial; what is mandatory in one state might be unnecessary in another. For instance, some states require more frequent filings, additional state-specific tax declarations, or other unique documentation. This diversity means that a one-size-fits-all approach to compliance is not only ineffective but potentially risky.

To navigate this complex landscape, leverage resources provided by state government websites, which offer detailed guidance on compliance requirements. These portals typically provide not only the forms and submission guidelines needed but also contact information for state offices where you can seek clarification on any unclear requirements. Additionally, consider the value of legal consultation, particularly if your LLC operates across multiple states. A compliance attorney can provide tailored advice and ensure that your business meets all multi-state obligations, safeguarding your operations against inadvertent legal breaches.

Regular Compliance Audits

Conducting regular compliance audits is akin to routine health check-ups for your LLC. These audits involve a systematic review of your business's adherence to legal standards and internal policies. The goal is to identify and address potential compliance issues before they escalate into legal problems. Schedule these audits at least annually, though more frequent reviews may be necessary depending on the nature of your business and the complexity of regulatory changes.

During an audit, review your business's legal documents, internal procedures, and compliance records. Check for consistency between your operations and the legal requirements that apply to your LLC. This might include verifying that your employee policies are in line with labor laws, your business licenses are up to date, and your tax filings are accurate and timely. If discrepancies are found, prioritize them based on risk and implement corrective actions swiftly. Regular audits not only help you maintain legal compliance but also instill confidence among your stakeholders, affirming your commitment to operational integrity and ethical business practices.

As you implement these strategies, remember that managing legal compliance is not a static task but a dynamic process that requires ongoing attention and adaptation. By establishing rigorous compliance practices, you not only protect your business from legal pitfalls but also position it for sustainable growth and success in the ever-evolving business landscape.

Protecting Your Personal Assets: LLCs and Liability

One of the most significant advantages of forming a Limited Liability Company (LLC) is the legal protection it offers your personal assets. This structure acts as a legal shield, separating your personal finances from the debts and liabilities of your business. Essentially, if your LLC faces a lawsuit or incurs debt, your personal assets—like your home, car, and savings—remain protected. This separation is often referred to as the "corporate veil," and maintaining it is crucial for the protection it offers.

The principle behind this protection lies in the legal identity of the LLC. Unlike sole proprietorships or partnerships, where the owners and the business are legally the same, an LLC is recognized as a separate legal entity. This distinction means creditors can pursue the assets of the LLC but not the personal assets of its members. For instance, if your LLC fails to repay a loan, only the assets of the business could be targeted by creditors, not your personal possessions. Similarly, in legal disputes involving contracts or business operations, your personal assets are typically out of reach in judgments against your LLC. This protection not only provides peace of mind but also encourages entrepreneurship by mitigating personal financial risk.

Maintaining the Corporate Veil

Maintaining the corporate veil involves more than just the initial setup of your LLC; it requires ongoing diligence to ensure that the separation between personal and business finances is clear and evident. One foundational practice is not commingling funds. This means keeping personal finances and business finances in separate bank accounts and ensuring that all transactions are clearly designated as either personal or business. Paying personal expenses from a business account or vice versa can blur the lines between personal and business finances, potentially jeopardizing the liability protection of the LLC. It's crucial to consistently document that the business is operating as a separate entity with its own assets and liabilities.

Real-life examples abound where the failure to adhere to these formalities resulted in significant personal financial loss. For instance, consider a small business owner who, for convenience, regularly used his business account to cover personal expenses. When his business faced financial difficulties, creditors were able to pierce the corporate veil, arguing that he was treating the LLC as an extension of his personal finances. The court agreed, rendering him personally liable for the business's debts. Such situations underscore the importance of meticulous financial management and adherence to legal protocols that reinforce the separation of your business and personal finances.

Advanced Strategies for Protection

For those seeking additional layers of protection, more advanced strategies can be employed. Forming holding companies or establishing multiple LLCs for different facets of your business operations can further shield your personal assets. A holding company owns other companies and typically does not have operations of its own. Its primary purpose is to control and manage the assets of its subsidiaries, providing an additional layer of liability protection. For example, if one subsidiary faces a lawsuit, the assets in the other subsidiaries or the holding company itself are usually protected. Similarly, using separate LLCs for different projects or properties can isolate the risks associated with each, preventing a liability issue in one part of your business from affecting the others.

Intellectual Property Considerations

In today's innovation-driven market, intellectual property (IP) represents one of the most valuable assets a business can hold. It encompasses a wide range of creations, from logos and corporate identity materials to product designs, original writings, and proprietary technologies. Understanding what constitutes intellectual property within your business is the first step toward leveraging these assets for competitive advantage and long-term success.

Types of Intellectual Property

Trademarks: These include any symbols, names, or phrases that distinguish your products or services from others. They are essential for brand recognition and customer loyalty.

Copyrights: These protect original works of authorship, such as books, articles, music, and artwork. While copyright protection is automatic upon creation, registering the copyright with the United States Copyright Office can provide additional legal benefits.

Patents: Patents shield inventions or discoveries that offer new technical solutions or improvements to existing products. The registration process through the United States Patent and Trademark Office (USPTO) is more involved and includes a thorough examination of the invention for novelty and non-obviousness.

Trade Secrets: These encompass practices, designs, formulas, processes, or collections of information that are not generally known or readily ascertainable, granting a business an economic advantage over competitors.

Protecting Your Intellectual Property

Proper registration of these intellectual properties is crucial. For trademarks, registration with the USPTO provides legal protection against unauthorized use that could cause confusion among consumers. Copyright registration, while not mandatory, offers significant advantages in enforcing rights. Patent registration not only protects inventions but can also enhance your business's credibility.

The benefits of registering your IP cannot be overstated. It deters potential infringement, enhances the appeal of your business to investors and potential buyers, and can significantly increase your company's valuation. By proactively protecting your intellectual property, you ensure that your innovations and creations remain unique to your business, fostering growth and maintaining your competitive edge.

Engaging Professionals

Implementing these strategies, while potentially complex, offers robust solutions for asset protection and risk management, especially for businesses with significant assets or those operating in higher-risk industries. It's advisable to seek the guidance of legal professionals who specialize in business and corporate law to ensure compliance with state regulations and maximize the protective benefits of your IP strategy.

Through these measures, you can fortify the defenses of your LLC, safeguarding not only your personal assets but also ensuring the longevity and stability of your business. Remember, the strength of your asset protection strategies significantly influences your business's capacity to weather legal challenges and financial downturns, securing not just your business's future but also your peace of mind.

Enforcing Intellectual Property Rights

When it comes to enforcing IP rights, vigilance is key. Continuously monitor the use of your intellectual property to detect any infringement early. If you discover that your IP rights are being violated, the first step is often to issue a cease and desist letter to the infringer. This letter serves as a formal request for the infringer to stop unauthorized activity and avoid legal action. However, if the infringement persists, litigation may become necessary. In such cases, consulting with an IP attorney is advisable. An attorney can offer expert guidance and represent your interests in court, helping you navigate the complexities of IP law and work towards a resolution, whether through negotiated settlements or court judgments.

Your intellectual property is not just a legal asset; it is also a crucial component of your business strategy. Properly managed, it can provide a significant competitive edge. For example, a well-known trademark can become synonymous with quality in the consumer's mind, driving sales and building brand loyalty. Patents can prevent competitors from using your innovations, allowing you to capture and maintain market share. Copyrights protect your creative outputs, ensuring competitors cannot undercut you by reproducing your original work. Furthermore, the strategic use of IP can attract partnerships, business opportunities, and even potential buyers, all of which can lead to new markets and revenue streams. By integrating IP considerations into your business planning and development strategies, you ensure that these assets contribute to your growth and profitability, securing not just your current operations but also paving the way for future expansion and success.

In this dynamic business environment, where innovation and uniqueness are paramount, understanding and strategically managing your intellectual property is imperative. It not only protects your creations but also enhances your market position, operational capabilities, and overall business valuation. As you continue to innovate and expand your business horizons, keep intellectual property rights management at the core of your strategic planning to ensure you fully capitalize on your intangible assets.

Handling Legal Disputes as an LLC

Navigating the complexities of legal disputes requires a proactive approach to minimize risks and manage conflicts effectively when they arise. As an LLC owner, it's crucial to understand that while disputes are often inevitable in business, their impact can be significantly mitigated with the right preventive strategies and dispute resolution mechanisms in place.

Clear Contract Terms: Starting with clear contract terms is essential. All agreements you enter into as a business—whether with customers, suppliers, or partners—should be documented formally and explicitly. Clear contracts outline the rights, responsibilities, and expectations of all parties involved, serving as your first line of defense against potential disputes. They ensure that everyone is on the same page from the outset and provide a solid basis for resolving misunderstandings before they escalate into more serious conflicts.

Navigating the complexities of legal disputes requires a proactive approach to minimize risks and manage conflicts effectively when they arise. As an LLC owner, it's crucial to understand that while disputes are often inevitable in business, their impact can be significantly mitigated with the right preventive strategies and dispute resolution mechanisms in place.

Clear Contract Terms: Starting with clear contract terms is essential. All agreements you enter into as a business—whether with customers, suppliers, or partners—should be documented formally and explicitly. Clear contracts outline the rights, responsibilities, and expectations of all parties involved, serving as your first line of defense against potential disputes. They ensure that everyone is on the same page from the outset and provide a solid basis for resolving misunderstandings before they escalate into more serious conflicts.

Proper Customer Communication: Another critical preventive strategy is proper customer communication. Regular and transparent communication can prevent many disputes related to unmet customer expectations. Ensure that your communication channels are open and accessible, and make it a policy to address queries and concerns promptly and effectively. This proactive approach can help build trust and clarify any uncertainties before they lead to conflicts.

Dispute Resolution Clauses: Integrating dispute resolution clauses in your contracts can be invaluable. These clauses typically specify how disputes will be handled, including the steps to follow before resorting to legal action, such as mandatory mediation or arbitration. By having these clauses in place, you can avoid the time and expense of court proceedings and resolve disputes more quickly and amicably.

Small Claims Courts: When disputes do arise, small claims courts can be a valuable resource for resolving them efficiently and cost-effectively, particularly when the dispute involves relatively small amounts, typically ranging from a few thousand dollars up to a limit set by state law. These courts are designed to be user-friendly, with simplified rules and procedures so that non-lawyers can effectively present their cases. This makes small claims courts an ideal venue for resolving minor disputes without the need for extensive legal representation. The process generally involves filing a claim with the court, after which a hearing is scheduled. Both parties present their case, and a judge makes a ruling. While specifics can vary by state, the general process is designed to be straightforward and accessible, making it a practical option for many small business owners.

Alternative Dispute Resolution: Alternative dispute resolution (ADR) methods, such as mediation and arbitration, offer additional pathways to resolving disputes without the need for a court trial. Mediation involves a neutral third party who helps the disputing parties find a mutually acceptable solution. It's a flexible process that can be tailored to the needs of the parties involved and often leads to solutions that preserve business relationships. Arbitration, on the other hand, involves an arbitrator who listens to both sides and then makes a decision that is usually binding. Both methods are less formal than traditional court proceedings and can be faster and less expensive. Including provisions for mediation and arbitration in business contracts can ensure that these methods are used before considering litigation.

This not only saves time and resources but also keeps disputes private and can preserve goodwill between parties.

Legal Representation: In situations where disputes cannot be resolved through these means, or when the complexity of the issue demands specialized knowledge, seeking legal representation becomes necessary. The key to effective legal representation is selecting the right attorney for your business's needs. Look for lawyers who specialize in business or contract law and who have experience with businesses similar to yours. Consider factors such as the attorney's familiarity with your industry, their approach to client communication, and their track record of success in resolving disputes.

Managing Legal Costs: Once you have selected an attorney, managing legal costs becomes a priority. Discuss fees upfront and consider different billing options, such as flat fees for specific services or retainer agreements. Effective communication with your attorney about your expectations and budget can prevent surprises and ensure that you get the most value out of your legal representation.

Insurance Needs for Your LLC

Navigating the complexities of insurance for your LLC can feel daunting, yet it's a critical step in safeguarding your business's future. The process begins with a thorough assessment of your specific insurance needs, which can vary widely depending on factors such as the nature of your business, its size, and its geographical location. For instance, a tech startup might prioritize cyber liability insurance due to the high risk of data breaches, while a construction business may find immense value in comprehensive general liability insurance to cover onsite accidents.

Risk Assessment: Begin by evaluating the key risks associated with your business activities. Consider potential scenarios that could disrupt operations or impose significant financial burdens. This proactive risk assessment forms the backbone of your insurance strategy, ensuring that you are prepared for potential liabilities.

Types of Business Insurance: Once you have identified these risks, the next step is to explore the types of business insurance available to mitigate these exposures:

General Liability Insurance: This is almost universally necessary as it protects against claims of bodily injury or property damage inflicted by your business operations.

Professional Liability Insurance: Also known as errors and omissions insurance, this coverage is crucial for businesses that provide services or advice, as it protects against claims of negligence or inadequate work.

Property Insurance: Essential if your business owns physical assets like office space, equipment, or inventory, property insurance covers damage from fire, theft, or natural disasters.

Workers' Compensation Insurance: For businesses with employees, this insurance is not only advisable but also legally required in most states, covering medical costs and lost wages for work-related injuries or illnesses.

Choosing the Right Insurance Provider: Selecting the right insurance provider is just as important as determining the correct type of coverage. Start by gathering quotes from multiple insurers to compare costs and coverage details. However, the decision should not be driven by price alone. Delve into the insurer's reputation by reviewing ratings and customer feedback, which can provide insights into their reliability and the quality of their customer service.

Understand the terms of each policy thoroughly—know what is covered and, just as importantly, what is not. This understanding will help you avoid gaps in coverage that could leave your business vulnerable. Additionally, consider the insurer's expertise in your industry; providers familiar with your specific sector will likely offer tailored coverage options that meet your unique needs.

Providers that specialize in your business sector may offer more tailored coverage options and risk management services. Regular reviews and updates of your insurance coverage are essential as your business evolves. Changes such as the expansion of your operations, the acquisition of new assets, or shifts in regulatory requirements can all impact your insurance needs. Schedule annual reviews of your policies to assess whether your existing coverage aligns with your current business profile or if adjustments are necessary. These reviews are also an opportune time to reassess your business risks and explore new insurance products that may have become available.

Insurance is more than just a regulatory requirement or a safety net; it is an integral component of your business strategy, protecting not only your financial assets but also the people who contribute to your business every day. By carefully assessing your needs, choosing the right coverage, and maintaining a relationship with a reputable provider, you ensure that your business can withstand the challenges it may face, allowing you to focus on growth and success.

As we conclude this chapter on legal compliance and risk management, reflect on the importance of a proactive approach to these areas. By understanding and managing your compliance obligations, protecting your assets, securing your intellectual property, resolving disputes effectively, and choosing the right insurance, you lay a strong foundation for your business. These efforts not only safeguard your operations but also position your company for future opportunities and challenges.

In the next chapter, we will explore growth and scaling strategies, helping you build on this foundation and expand your business successfully.

FIVE

Growth and Scaling Strategies

As you stand at the threshold of expanding your LLC, the landscape ahead is vibrant with opportunities, each path offering unique growth and challenges. Just as a gardener nurtures various plants, understanding the ecosystem of your market is crucial to ensuring that your business not only grows but thrives. In this chapter, we will delve into the fertile ground of effective marketing strategies, planting seeds that will help your business flourish in a competitive environment.

You'll learn to identify the rich soils of your target markets, cultivate a robust marketing plan, and tend to the ongoing needs of your campaigns through diligent tracking and adjustments. This journey into marketing is not merely about spreading the word about your business; it's about ensuring that every message resonates deeply with your audience, transforming potential leads into loyal customers.

Effective Marketing Strategies for New LLCs

Identifying Target Markets

Embarking on a marketing journey without a clear understanding of your target market is akin to setting sail without a compass. The first step in any successful marketing strategy is to clearly identify and understand who your customers are. This process involves more than just knowing demographic information like age, gender, and location. To truly connect with your audience, you must delve into psychographic and behavioral characteristics.

Psychographics encompass personality traits, values, interests, and lifestyles, while behavioral characteristics focus on how customers interact with products, including purchasing behaviors and brand loyalty.

Start by gathering data through market research, which can include surveys, focus groups, and analysis of existing customer data. Use this information to create detailed buyer personas—semi-fictional characters that represent your ideal customers. These personas should encompass not only demographic and psychographic details but also the challenges and pain points that your product or service can address. Understanding these nuances allows you to tailor your marketing messages to resonate more deeply with potential customers, enhancing the effectiveness of your campaigns.

Developing a Marketing Plan

With a clear understanding of your target market, the next step is to develop a comprehensive marketing plan. This plan serves as a blueprint for how you will communicate with your market and achieve your marketing goals. Begin with thorough market research to gauge your competition and the overall landscape. This research should inform your SWOT analysis—identifying strengths, weaknesses, opportunities, and threats related to your business.

Next, set clear marketing goals. These should be specific, measurable, achievable, relevant, and time-bound (SMART). For instance, instead of a vague goal like "increase visibility," a SMART goal would be "increase website traffic by 30% within three months." Following this, outline the strategies and tactics to achieve these goals, which could include content marketing, social media advertising, email campaigns, or traditional advertising like radio or print ads.

Your marketing budget is a critical component of the plan. It should detail the costs associated with each tactic and project the return on investment (ROI) for these activities. This budgetary planning ensures that you allocate resources effectively, maximizing your marketing spend for the best possible outcomes.

Utilizing Digital Marketing Tools

In today's digital landscape, leveraging online marketing tools is not just advantageous but essential. Digital marketing encompasses a range of strategies, including social media marketing, email marketing, content marketing, and search engine optimization (SEO). Each of these tools offers unique benefits:

Social Media Marketing: Enhances your brand's visibility and facilitates direct engagement with customers.

Email Marketing: Enables personalized communication and promotions, driving both customer acquisition and retention.

Content Marketing: Establishes your brand as a thought leader by providing valuable information that attracts and retains customers.

Search Engine Optimization (SEO): Improves your website's visibility in search engine results, which is critical for driving organic traffic.

Specific Strategies for Digital Marketing Channels

For each digital marketing channel, develop specific strategies that align with your overall marketing goals. Utilize tools like Hootsuite for social media management, Mailchimp for email campaigns, and Google Analytics for SEO and website performance analysis. These tools not only facilitate the implementation of your strategies but also enable you to monitor and optimize them based on real-time data.

Tracking and Adjusting Marketing Efforts

The landscape of marketing is ever-evolving, making flexibility key to maintaining the effectiveness of your campaigns. Employ analytics tools to track the performance of all your marketing activities. Focus on metrics such as:

- Website traffic

- Conversion rates

- Engagement rates on social media

- Effectiveness of different content types

Analyzing these metrics provides insights into what's working and what isn't, allowing you to make informed decisions about adjusting your strategies. For instance, if data reveals that your email campaigns have high open rates but low conversion rates, you might revise your call-to-action or the offers included in the emails. Similarly, if certain blog posts attract significantly more traffic, it indicates topics that resonate with your audience, guiding your future content creation.

Regular review meetings—whether monthly or quarterly—can be beneficial for discussing these insights and planning adjustments. This iterative process ensures your marketing efforts remain fresh, relevant, and effective, continually adapting to meet the needs of your market and the goals of your LLC.

In this chapter, we explored foundational strategies to effectively market your new LLC. As you implement these strategies, remember that marketing is not a static process but a dynamic interaction with your target audience. Your ability to adapt and evolve your strategies based on ongoing data and feedback will be key to sustaining and growing your customer base, ultimately contributing to the long-term success and scalability of your business.

Hiring Your First Employees

When the time comes to expand your team, understanding the legal and practical aspects of hiring is crucial not only to find the right candidates but also to ensure compliance with various employment laws. Hiring your first employees marks a significant milestone in the growth of your LLC, transforming it from a solo venture into a collaborative business.

This process begins with a clear comprehension of the legal requirements associated with employment, including tax regulations and workers' compensation obligations. Each state has its own set of laws governing employment, including:

- Minimum wage requirements

- Anti-discrimination laws

- Safety regulations

Additionally, you'll need to register with your state labor department and set up systems to handle payroll taxes, which include withholding state and federal taxes and paying Social Security and Medicare. Ensuring compliance with these laws not only protects you from potential legal issues but also establishes a fair and professional working environment.

Creating Effective Job Descriptions

Creating effective job descriptions is your next critical step. This often underestimated task is vital for attracting the right talent and clarifying expectations for both employer and employee. A well-crafted job description serves as a tool to communicate the duties and responsibilities of the position clearly. It should outline necessary skills and qualifications, the role's objectives, and how it fits into the larger operations of your business.

To write a clear and concise job description, start by detailing the day-to-day responsibilities expected of the role. Be specific to avoid future misunderstandings. Next, list the required skills and experiences, distinguishing between those that are essential and those that are preferred. This distinction can help widen your pool of applicants. Additionally, describe the role's impact on your business, as this can attract candidates looking for more than just a job—they want a place where they can make a difference.

Interviewing and Selecting Candidates

The process of interviewing and selecting candidates is where your preparations begin to materialize into potential hires. This stage is crucial and requires a structured approach to ensure fairness and effectiveness. Start by screening resumes based on the criteria set out in your job descriptions, simplifying the process of identifying qualified candidates.

During interviews, use a mix of standard and job-specific questions to assess not only competencies but also the compatibility of candidates with your company culture. Employing behavioral interview techniques—where candidates describe past job experiences and behaviors—can provide deep insights into their skills and problem-solving abilities. After interviews, consider conducting background checks as necessary, always with the candidates' consent, to confirm their qualifications and ensure security within your business operations.

Onboarding New Employees

Once you have selected your new team members, the focus shifts to integrating them into your business through a structured onboarding process. Effective onboarding is essential; it helps new hires understand their roles and responsibilities and aligns them with your business's values and goals. Begin by preparing an onboarding packet that includes all necessary paperwork, an employee handbook, and detailed plans for their first few weeks. This packet should help them feel informed and welcomed.

The first days are crucial; ensure that you have planned a comprehensive introduction to the team, their new workspace, and the tools they'll use. Setting up initial training sessions to cover operational procedures and role-specific tasks can also smooth this transition. Regular check-ins during the first few months can help address any concerns they might have and reinforce their understanding of their role and contributions to the team.

Conclusion

By meticulously planning and executing each of these steps—from understanding legal hiring requirements to onboarding new employees—you lay a solid foundation for building a strong, effective team. This process not only enhances the operational capacity of your LLC but also fosters a workplace culture that attracts and retains top talent, driving the growth and success of your business.

Developing a Customer Retention Strategy

Customer retention is vital for the sustainable growth of your LLC. Retaining existing customers is not only more cost-effective but also provides a stable and predictable revenue stream, unlike the ongoing efforts required to attract new ones. Studies show that increasing retention rates by just 5% can boost profits by 25% to 95%. This impressive growth is due to the lower costs associated with serving current customers—who are more likely to make repeat purchases—compared to the higher expense of converting new prospects. Additionally, loyal customers often serve as brand advocates, spreading word-of-mouth recommendations that bring in new business without additional marketing costs.

Personalization plays a critical role in building strong customer relationships. In an era saturated with generic marketing messages, personalized service is a key differentiator. Use customer data to tailor your communications and offerings. For instance, send customized emails that address customers by name and recommend products based on their past purchases, making your messages feel more relevant and engaging. This personalized approach can extend beyond email to customer service. Equip your team with access to each customer's purchase history and prior interactions, enabling them to provide solutions tailored to individual needs, which enhances satisfaction and improves the overall experience.

Regular communication is another cornerstone of customer retention. Keep customers updated about new products, promotions, and company news through newsletters, social media, and personalized emails. However, ensure these communications offer real value rather than just pushing sales. Include useful content like industry insights, tips, or news that benefit your customers. Creating a feedback loop is also essential for maintaining strong relationships. Encourage customers to share feedback on their experiences and suggest improvements. This not only provides valuable insights for your business but also makes customers feel heard and valued.

Loyalty programs are a proven strategy to enhance retention by rewarding repeat business. These programs incentivize customers to make more purchases, increasing their lifetime value. When designing a loyalty program, make sure the rewards are appealing and attainable. For example, a points-based system allows customers to earn points for every purchase, which they can redeem for discounts, products, or exclusive perks. A tiered system is another option, where customers unlock additional rewards like free shipping or early access to new products as they spend more. Well-designed loyalty programs foster deeper engagement and encourage long-term customer loyalty.

Exceptional Customer Service: The Cornerstone of Retention

Exceptional customer service is arguably the most critical element of a successful retention strategy. It can determine whether a customer remains loyal or switches to a competitor. Train your customer service team to handle inquiries and complaints with efficiency and empathy. Empower them to resolve issues quickly, whether that means offering a discount or providing a complimentary product to address a service failure. This proactive approach can turn a negative experience into a positive one, fostering customer loyalty.

Additionally, ensure that your customer service is easily accessible across multiple channels, such as phone, email, live chat, and social media. This multi-channel approach ensures that customers can reach you whenever and however they prefer, making it more convenient for them to seek assistance when needed.

By implementing strategies such as personalized service, regular communication, an appealing loyalty program, and exceptional customer service, you can create a comprehensive retention strategy that not only keeps customers returning but also turns them into advocates for your brand. This approach not only stabilizes your revenue but also builds a loyal customer base, which can organically attract new clients and contribute to the ongoing growth of your LLC.

Exploring Expansion Opportunities

Once your LLC stabilizes with a consistent income and engaged customer base, the next step may involve considering expansion. Growth isn't just about increasing sales—it's about ensuring your business remains adaptable in a rapidly changing market. To effectively explore expansion opportunities, start with thorough market research to assess current conditions and identify emerging trends. This process goes beyond understanding current customer needs; it also involves anticipating future demands and spotting gaps your business can fill.

Tools like customer surveys, market reports, and competitor analysis can provide valuable insights.

A SWOT analysis (Strengths, Weaknesses, Opportunities, and Threats) is another key tool to guide your expansion decisions. It helps you evaluate your internal capabilities and external market conditions, giving you a clear picture of where your business currently stands and where it can grow. Additionally, feasibility studies are essential during this phase. These studies assess the practicality and profitability of new ventures, helping to minimize the risks associated with expansion. Factors such as economic viability, technical requirements, legal considerations, and timelines are all analyzed to ensure that the expansion is both realistic and sustainable.

Exploring Diversification Strategies for Growth

Once you have a solid understanding of your growth potential, exploring diversification strategies can provide new pathways to expand your market reach and revenue streams. One common approach is introducing complementary products or services. For example, a coffee shop might start offering baking classes, leveraging its existing customer base and resources. Another option is market diversification, which involves entering new markets, whether geographically or by targeting different demographics within your current operational areas.

Vertical integration is also a strategic consideration, where you take control of multiple stages of the supply chain. For instance, a manufacturer might acquire one of its suppliers to reduce costs and gain more control over production. Each of these strategies has its own challenges and benefits, and success depends on selecting the one that aligns best with your business goals and market conditions.

Consider successful diversifications in your industry for inspiration. For example, a tech company that initially focused on software might expand into hardware to provide integrated solutions, capturing a larger market share and increasing customer loyalty to its ecosystem.

Franchising and Licensing as Expansion Strategies

Franchising and licensing are powerful strategies that can offer lucrative opportunities for expansion. Franchising allows you to grow your brand's presence without the substantial capital costs typically associated with corporate expansion. As the franchisor, you grant franchisees the license to operate under your brand name, using your established business model. This can lead to rapid growth and additional revenue through franchise fees and royalties. However, maintaining consistent quality and brand standards across franchises can be a challenge.

Licensing, on the other hand, involves granting another company the rights to manufacture and sell products under your brand or use your intellectual property. This method allows you to expand your brand's reach with minimal investment. However, there are risks, such as losing control over product quality or diluting your brand's identity.

Partnerships and Collaborations for Strategic Growth

Partnerships and collaborations offer another strategic growth avenue by combining the strengths and resources of both parties to achieve shared goals. For example, a small fashion brand might partner with a larger retailer to access a broader market, benefiting from the larger brand's established distribution channels and customer base.

To ensure successful partnerships, it's essential to have clear agreements in place that outline each partner's contributions, responsibilities, and profit-sharing structure. Regular communication and alignment on objectives are key to making these collaborations work.

Thoughtful Implementation of Expansion Strategies

By carefully assessing and implementing these expansion strategies—whether through diversification, franchising, licensing, or partnerships—you can significantly enhance your business's growth potential and strengthen its competitive edge. Successful expansion requires strategic planning, thorough market research, and judicious investment. Always stay grounded in your business's core values and commitments to customers. As you explore these opportunities, focus on delivering exceptional value and maintaining the high standards that have been integral to your success so far.

Leveraging Technology for Business Efficiency

In today's fast-paced business environment, the strategic use of technology can be a game-changer for your LLC. From streamlining operations to enhancing customer interactions, technology offers a wide array of tools designed to increase efficiency and fuel business growth. The first step in harnessing this potential is assessing your business's technological needs. Begin by evaluating current processes and identifying areas where technology could deliver significant improvements. For instance, if manual inventory management is taking up excessive time, an automated inventory management system could be the answer. Similarly, if tracking customer interactions and sales leads is becoming overwhelming, a Customer Relationship Management (CRM) system could streamline these tasks, ensuring no opportunities are missed.

Moreover, consider how technology can optimize your accounting practices. While traditional accounting methods may be reliable, they are often time-consuming and prone to human error. Implementing accounting software can automate tasks like generating invoices and preparing financial reports, allowing you to manage your finances with greater accuracy and less effort. Prioritize these needs based on their potential impact on your business, helping you focus on the technologies that will offer the greatest benefits.

Selecting the Right Technology

Investing in the right technology is essential for realizing these benefits, but with so many options available, the selection process can feel overwhelming. Focus on tools that align with your business goals and fit your budget. Research the technologies that other businesses in your industry use, paying close attention to those praised for reliability and cost-effectiveness. Read reviews, watch demos, and, if possible, use trial versions to understand how these tools could function within your business.

When evaluating solutions, consider both their immediate and future utility. Opt for scalable systems that can grow alongside your business. Additionally, assess the level of customer support provided by vendors, as reliable support can minimize downtime and frustration during implementation.

Once you've selected the appropriate tools, plan your investment carefully. In addition to the initial purchase cost, account for ongoing expenses such as maintenance fees, subscription costs, and any required hardware or infrastructure.

Implementing Technology Effectively

The successful implementation of new technology requires thorough planning and execution. Begin by preparing your team for the upcoming changes. Clearly explain the benefits of the new technology and how it will impact their daily tasks. Proper training is key to ensuring that everyone can use the new tools effectively. Depending on the complexity of the system, you may want to hire an external trainer or work with the vendor to provide comprehensive training sessions.

During the implementation phase, keep communication channels open. Encourage your team to provide feedback and report any issues they encounter. This input is crucial for troubleshooting and refining the process. Be prepared for challenges, as technology integration often comes with unexpected hurdles that may require adjustments to workflows or additional training.

Ongoing Evaluation and Adjustment

Technology is not a one-time solution; it requires ongoing evaluation to ensure it continues to meet your business's needs. Establish a system for regular review meetings where you can assess the technology's performance, gather feedback from users, and make necessary adjustments. This proactive approach will help you maximize the benefits of your technology investments, ensuring they continue to enhance your business's efficiency and drive growth.

Evaluating Technology ROI

Understanding the return on investment (ROI) of your technology implementations is crucial for justifying expenses and planning future investments. When evaluating ROI, consider both tangible and intangible benefits. Tangible benefits directly impact your bottom line, such as cost savings from increased efficiency or increased sales through improved customer service. Intangible benefits, while harder to measure in financial terms, can significantly affect your business as well. These might include enhanced employee satisfaction from streamlined task management or strengthened customer loyalty resulting from superior service.

To calculate ROI, begin by quantifying the financial benefits derived from the technology. This could involve tracking changes in revenue, reductions in operational costs, or decreases in your customer churn rate. Next, subtract the total cost of the technology, which includes the initial setup, subscription fees, and any ongoing maintenance costs. The result is your net return. Divide this figure by the total cost of the technology to determine the ROI percentage. A positive ROI indicates that the technology has been a valuable investment, while a negative ROI suggests that the benefits may not justify the costs.

While intangible benefits may not be directly reflected in your ROI calculation, they can have a lasting positive impact on your business's reputation and growth potential. These factors should be considered when deciding whether to continue, expand, or modify your technology investments.

In this chapter, you've explored how to strategically leverage technology to enhance your business operations' efficiency and effectiveness. From identifying areas ripe for technological improvement to assessing the ROI of your investments, each step ensures that your technological infrastructure supports and accelerates business growth. As you continue integrating and optimizing technology within your business, remember that the ultimate goal is to build a resilient, adaptable, and increasingly efficient enterprise.

In the next chapter, you'll dive into advanced financial management strategies that can further solidify your business foundation and propel it toward sustained success and profitability.

If you found this book helpful in starting your entrepreneurial journey, I would be incredibly grateful if you could take a moment to leave a positive review. Your feedback not only encourages me, but it also helps others who are seeking the confidence and guidance to finally take the leap into business ownership. By sharing your experience, you're helping fellow entrepreneurs find the tools they need to succeed and start their own journey with clarity and confidence. Thank you for being a part of this mission!

CHAPTER
SIX

Advanced Financial Management

Navigating Advanced Financial Management for Your LLC

Managing the financial intricacies of an LLC extends far beyond basic bookkeeping or handling day-to-day transactions. As your business evolves, so must your financial strategies. This chapter delves into advanced financial management techniques that not only safeguard your current assets but also optimize your business's future financial health. From exploring legal tax loopholes to navigating multi-state taxation, these insights are designed to elevate your financial acumen, empowering you to take full control of your financial destiny.

Advanced Tax Strategies for LLCs

Utilizing Legal Tax Loopholes

Taxation is often viewed as a complex maze of rules and regulations, which can be daunting for many LLC owners. However, hidden within these complexities are opportunities—legal tax savings avenues that can significantly enhance your LLC's financial efficiency. These opportunities typically come in the form of deductions, allowances, and credits, embedded within the tax code to incentivize specific business activities.

For instance, frequently overlooked deductions like home office use or business travel are not just perks; they are strategic tax relief options for businesses operating in today's dynamic environments. Likewise, depreciation allowances on high-value equipment can substantially reduce your taxable income, improving cash flow. Additionally, tax credits for research and development activities or green energy initiatives provide direct, dollar-for-dollar reductions in tax liability, boosting profit margins.

Effectively navigating these legal strategies requires a thorough understanding of the tax code, often in partnership with a seasoned tax professional. By leveraging these legitimate avenues, you can minimize your tax burden while aligning your business practices with activities that are not only encouraged by the tax code but also beneficial for your LLC's overall financial strategy and long-term growth.

Maximizing Benefits from Pass-Through Taxation

One of the most significant advantages of operating your business as an LLC is pass-through taxation. This structure allows the profits of your business to "pass through" to your personal tax return, avoiding the double taxation that corporations often face. However, maximizing this benefit requires strategic planning to ensure it aligns with your personal financial goals.

One key strategy is managing the amount of income that passes through to your personal taxes by adjusting your salary if you actively work in the business. Paying yourself a reasonable salary reduces the LLC's profits that pass through to your personal tax return, which could potentially lower your overall tax bracket. Additionally, consider contributing to retirement plans or health savings accounts (HSAs), which not only lower your taxable income but also improve your long-term financial security.

These approaches require careful planning and a comprehensive understanding of both business and personal tax implications. Consulting with tax professionals who can offer tailored advice based on your specific situation is essential to fully capitalize on these strategies.

Advanced Depreciation Techniques

Depreciation is a powerful tax-planning tool, enabling businesses to account for asset costs over their useful lives. Advanced depreciation methods like accelerated depreciation and Section 179 deductions can be especially beneficial for LLCs. Accelerated depreciation allows for larger write-offs in the early years of an asset's life, providing significant tax relief and improving short-term cash flow.

Section 179 offers even more immediate benefits, permitting the full deduction of qualifying business equipment in the year it is placed in service, up to a specified limit. These strategies reduce taxable income while encouraging investment in new technology and equipment, which can drive efficiency and productivity in your operations.

To leverage these techniques effectively, you need to stay current with tax law changes, as they directly impact the availability and benefits of these depreciation options. Regular consultations with tax advisors and investing in accounting software capable of handling complex depreciation calculations are advisable to maximize these opportunities.

Handling Multi-State Taxation

For LLCs operating in multiple states, managing tax obligations can be a complex endeavor. Each state has different rules regarding income apportionment, sales tax, and nexus—the level of business activity that triggers tax liability in a given state. Understanding these variations is critical to maintaining compliance and optimizing tax obligations across jurisdictions.

A common challenge is navigating the sales tax requirements in different states, particularly with the rise of online sales. It's essential to establish a system to track sales by state and understand the specific thresholds that trigger tax obligations. Likewise, income apportionment rules, which determine how much of your business income is taxable in each state, require careful calculation and strategic planning.

Employing accounting practices that accurately capture the sources of income and expenses by state can ensure correct tax filing and help avoid costly penalties. By developing a comprehensive multi-state tax strategy, your LLC can minimize tax liabilities while remaining compliant with all relevant regulations.

By implementing these advanced tax strategies, your LLC can not only comply with complex tax regulations but also take full advantage of legal opportunities to reduce tax liabilities. This proactive approach to financial management not only ensures compliance but also bolsters the financial health and growth potential of your business, positioning it for long-term success in an ever-evolving economic landscape.

Managing Cash Flow for Growth

Understanding and managing cash flow is like keeping your business's heart beating, particularly as you plan for growth and expansion. Advanced forecasting models and budgeting techniques are crucial for more than just maintaining day-to-day operations. They help align your financial strategies with long-term business goals. Sophisticated forecasting goes beyond simple trend analysis, incorporating variables like seasonal fluctuations, market trends, and potential changes in the economic environment.

Techniques such as rolling forecasts—which continuously update predictions based on new data—offer greater flexibility and accuracy than traditional annual budgets. These models anticipate future cash flow needs, ensuring your business has the resources to support initiatives and investments without compromising operational stability. For example, when launching a new product line, your cash flow forecast can help you determine the best timing for investments in marketing and production. It can also alert you to potential cash shortfalls, allowing you to adjust operations by delaying non-essential expenditures or securing additional funding.

This proactive financial planning not only protects your business from liquidity crises but also supports informed decision-making, empowering you to seize opportunities and navigate challenges effectively.

Streamlining Accounts Receivable and Payable

Effective management of accounts receivable and payable is another cornerstone of financial health. Beyond diligent bookkeeping, this requires strategic policies that accelerate cash inflows and carefully manage outflows to maintain a healthy balance. Negotiating favorable payment terms with both suppliers and clients can enhance cash flow significantly.

For instance, extending your payment terms with suppliers from 30 to 45 days provides more flexibility in managing cash outflows without harming relationships. On the flip side, offering slight discounts to customers for early invoice payments can accelerate inflows, improving your liquidity position. By streamlining these processes, you create a more stable cash flow that enables sustainable growth.

Invoice Factoring and Cash Reserves

Invoice factoring can be an effective tool for managing receivables, especially in businesses with long payment cycles. In this arrangement, you sell your invoices to a factoring company at a discount, and they take on the responsibility of collecting payments from your customers. While this results in receiving less than the full value of your invoices, the immediate influx of cash can outweigh the cost, particularly if it helps cover critical expenses like payroll or supplier payments. This method also prevents the need to rely on more expensive forms of credit.

Maintaining adequate cash reserves is another essential component of sound financial management. Cash reserves act as a buffer against unforeseen expenses or to capitalize on emerging opportunities. A general rule is to maintain reserves sufficient to cover three to six months of operating expenses, though this may vary depending on your business's risk profile, cash flow stability, and growth ambitions. Liquidity management strategies, such as keeping a line of credit open or investing in short-term liquid assets, can further enhance your ability to respond swiftly to financial needs. These strategies not only protect your business in downturns but also position you to seize opportunities as they arise, giving your LLC a competitive advantage.

Utilizing Financial Ratios for Strategic Decisions

Leveraging financial ratios can provide critical insights into your business's financial health, guiding your decision-making process. Two particularly insightful ratios are the quick ratio and the cash conversion cycle.

The quick ratio, calculated as **(cash + marketable securities + accounts receivable) / current liabilities**, measures your business's ability to meet short-term obligations using its most liquid assets. A strong quick ratio generally indicates good liquidity, but this must be balanced with an understanding of the cash conversion cycle, which tracks how long it takes for cash to return to your business after it has been spent on inventory and operating expenses.

Optimizing the cash conversion cycle by improving inventory management, accelerating receivables, and extending payables can significantly enhance cash flow. A shorter cash conversion cycle allows for smoother operations and supports sustainable growth. Mastering these financial ratios helps you make informed decisions that keep your LLC agile and resilient.

Securing Additional Funding

Equity financing can unlock significant growth opportunities for your LLC by exchanging business ownership for capital investment. This capital can come from various sources, each offering unique benefits and challenges. Venture capital firms, for example, typically focus on high-growth businesses with scalable models. In addition to funding, they often provide strategic advice and access to their networks, which can be invaluable for your business's expansion.

However, securing venture capital is a competitive process that demands a well-constructed business plan, clear evidence of growth potential, and a compelling pitch. Preparing for this journey requires thorough market research, a solid financial foundation, and readiness to negotiate the terms of investment while maintaining alignment with your long-term business goals.

Preparing to Approach Investors

Venture Capitalists

Approaching venture capitalists requires more than just a solid grasp of your financial metrics; it demands a compelling narrative that encapsulates your business's potential, market dynamics, and future vision. Your preparation should encompass detailed financial projections, comprehensive market analysis, and a clear outline of how the investment will be utilized to spur growth. Given that venture capitalists conduct thorough due diligence, it's essential to have a well-structured plan that not only highlights potential risks but also identifies market opportunities. This proactive approach can significantly enhance your credibility and appeal to investors.

Angel Investors

Conversely, angel investors are often high-net-worth individuals who seek to invest in startups at an earlier stage than venture capitalists. Interactions with angel investors tend to be more personal and less formal, providing a unique opportunity for new entrepreneurs to forge meaningful connections. Like their venture capital counterparts, angel investors offer not just financial backing but also their expertise and networks, which can be invaluable during the critical early phases of your business. When preparing for meetings with potential angel investors, focus on establishing a personal rapport, showcasing your passion and dedication, and clearly delineating your path to profitability.

Private Equity

Private equity represents another avenue for equity financing, primarily suited for more established companies looking to expand or restructure. Typically, private equity investors engage through buyouts, acquiring a significant stake or complete ownership of the company. They often take an active role in strategic management, aiming to increase the company's value before eventually selling it for a profit. Engaging with private equity firms necessitates a clear understanding of their investment criteria and a readiness to potentially relinquish some control over business decision-making.

Utilizing Debt Financing Wisely

Debt financing, unlike equity financing, does not involve selling a portion of your business. Instead, it entails borrowing funds to be repaid over time, usually with interest. This approach can be advantageous as it allows you to retain full ownership of your LLC; however, it requires diligent management to prevent cash flow constraints. Common methods of debt financing include securing loans, establishing lines of credit, or issuing bonds.

When seeking loans or lines of credit from banks or lending institutions, your business's credit history, financial stability, and the viability of your business plan will be closely scrutinized. Preparation is key: ensure your financial statements are accurate and up-to-date, your business plan is comprehensive, and you have a clear understanding of the funding amount required and its intended use. It's equally important to be aware of the loan terms, including interest rates, repayment schedules, and any covenants or conditions the lender may impose.

Negotiating Favorable Terms

Negotiating favorable financing terms relies heavily on the strength of your preparation and an understanding of the lender's perspective. Lenders want assurance that you have a solid repayment plan and that your business can generate sufficient cash flow to meet its obligations. Demonstrating a deep understanding of your market and presenting a clear risk mitigation strategy can sometimes help you secure better terms.

Grants and Non-Traditional Funding Sources

In addition to traditional debt and equity financing, various non-traditional funding sources can provide financial support without the burden of equity or debt repayments.

Government Grants

Government grants are often available for businesses contributing to economic development, innovation, or other societal benefits. These grants typically do not require repayment, making them highly attractive. However, they can be competitive and often come with specific restrictions on how the funds can be used.

Crowdfunding

Crowdfunding platforms offer a modern approach to raising capital by pooling small investments from a large number of people, usually via the internet. This method not only helps raise funds but also serves to validate your business idea and generate public interest. To prepare for a crowdfunding campaign, focus on creating compelling content and attractive rewards that motivate potential investors, along with a robust promotional strategy.

Industry-Specific Funds

Industry-specific funds are particularly valuable for businesses in specialized fields like technology, healthcare, or sustainable energy. These funds are typically provided by organizations aimed at promoting innovation within specific sectors. To secure funding from these sources, you need a thorough understanding of the industry, a clear demonstration of your innovation or added value, and alignment with the fund's objectives.

Preparing for Diligence Processes

Regardless of the funding source, the due diligence process is a critical step where potential financiers assess your business's viability and the credibility of your financial forecasts. Proper preparation involves organizing all essential business documents, including financial statements, contracts, business plans, and tax returns.

Transparency about potential risks and your plans to mitigate them is also crucial. Being well-prepared for due diligence means not only having your documentation in order but also being ready to answer in-depth questions about your business operations, market conditions, and competitive landscape. This level of preparedness can significantly influence the confidence financiers have in your business, impacting their decision to invest.

Advanced Financing Options

As you consider these advanced financing options, remember that each comes with its own nuances and requirements. The key is to carefully evaluate which options align best with your business goals and growth strategies, preparing meticulously for the engagement and negotiation processes involved. This strategic approach to securing additional funding will support your business's growth trajectory and help ensure its long-term financial stability.

Financial Planning for Long-Term Success

Strategic Financial Planning

Integrating financial planning with your business strategy goes beyond merely managing your finances; it's about setting a course that ensures every financial decision supports your broader business goals. Think of strategic financial planning as the process of aligning your business's financial goals with its long-term objectives, ensuring that every investment, expense, and revenue projection propels your business toward its envisioned future. This alignment requires a comprehensive understanding of your current position and a clear vision of where you want to be in five, ten, or even twenty years.

Start by defining clear, strategic financial goals that directly link to your business objectives. For example, if your aim is to expand market reach, your financial strategy might involve increasing the budget for marketing and sales efforts or investing in new product development. Ensure these goals are specific, measurable, achievable, relevant, and time-bound (SMART), allowing for seamless integration into your operational plans.

Once established, create a financial roadmap outlining the necessary steps to achieve these goals, including detailed budget forecasts, investment plans, and funding strategies. This strategic plan serves as your financial compass, guiding your business through the complexities of growth and market changes.

Your plan should be dynamic, allowing for adaptability in response to changes in the business environment or your strategic direction. Regular reviews—monthly, quarterly, or annually—enable you to adjust your financial plan based on internal developments and external economic conditions. This may involve recalibrating budget allocations, reevaluating investment strategies, or reshaping funding plans to align with your evolving objectives. An integrated, agile strategic financial plan not only helps navigate volatile economic waters but also ensures your business stays on course toward its long-term goals.

Risk Assessment and Management

Identifying and managing financial risks is crucial for safeguarding your business's assets and ensuring its long-term viability. Financial risks can arise from various sources, including market fluctuations, credit issues, operational failures, or unforeseen economic downturns. Effective risk management begins with a thorough assessment—identifying specific risks that could impact your business, evaluating their likelihood, and understanding their potential impact.

After identifying these risks, develop strategies to mitigate them. For instance, if market volatility poses a significant risk, consider diversifying your product lines or markets to reduce reliance on a single revenue source. To address credit risks, enhance your credit control processes by tightening credit terms or improving your follow-up procedures for debtors. Operational risks can be mitigated through improved infrastructure and investment in robust systems and processes that enhance efficiency and reduce failure likelihood.

Incorporating risk management into your financial planning involves allocating resources to handle potential risks. This may include creating contingency funds for emergencies, purchasing insurance to cover significant risks, or establishing lines of credit to ensure liquidity during tough times. Regularly reviewing and updating your risk management strategies is as vital as establishing them, ensuring their effectiveness as your business and the external environment evolve.

Investment Strategies for Growth

Investing your profits wisely is crucial for the sustained growth and expansion of your LLC. As your business generates profits, reinvesting a portion of these funds into growth-oriented activities can significantly propel your business forward. The investment options for LLCs can vary widely, depending on your business goals and risk tolerance.

Investment Avenues

- **Real Estate:** This can provide a steady income stream and potential for capital appreciation, making it suitable for businesses prioritizing stability.

- **Stocks**: Investing in stocks offers the potential for significant growth, aligning with faster growth objectives.

- **Bonds**: These add a stable, low-risk component to your investment portfolio, appealing to those focused on risk management.

Additionally, consider alternative investments such as venture capital or private equity. These can yield high returns and offer strategic advantages, such as partnerships with innovative startups or companies that complement your business operations.

Diversification and Portfolio Management

Developing a diversified investment portfolio is essential for managing risk and achieving balanced growth. By spreading investments across different asset classes, you can protect your business from significant losses if one investment underperforms. Regularly reviewing and adjusting your portfolio in response to market changes and shifts in your business strategy ensures that your investments continue to align with your overall objectives.

Succession Planning

Planning for the succession of your business is crucial for ensuring continuity and preserving its legacy. Whether due to retirement, incapacity, or the decision to hand over leadership to a successor, having a well-thought-out succession plan is essential. This plan should address not only who will take over the leadership of your business but also how the transition will be managed financially and legally.

Identifying Successors

Start by identifying potential successors—whether family members, business partners, or external candidates—and begin grooming them early. This might involve training them in various aspects of the business, involving them in strategic decisions, and gradually increasing their responsibilities.

Financial Strategies for Ownership Transfer

Ensure that your succession plan includes strategies for transferring ownership, which might involve buy-sell agreements, gifting shares, or selling the business. Each method has different financial and tax implications, so it's crucial to consult with financial and legal advisors to determine the most suitable strategy for your situation.

Legal Documentation

Legally, your succession plan should be documented in detail, outlining the terms of the succession, the roles and responsibilities of all parties involved, and the legal processes that will be followed during the transition. This legal documentation provides clarity and direction for the transition and helps prevent potential disputes or misunderstandings between the parties involved.

Exit Strategies: Selling Your LLC

When the time comes to sell your LLC—whether for retirement, capitalizing on your investment, or pursuing new ventures—the process involves much more than simply putting up a 'For Sale' sign. It requires meticulous preparation, strategic marketing, skillful negotiation, and careful handling of the transition to ensure both the continuity of the business and the preservation of its value. Understanding these stages and approaching each with careful planning can significantly influence the success of the sale and your satisfaction with the outcome.

Preparation for Sale

The preparation phase is fundamental, setting the stage for a successful sale. Start by accurately valuing your business, which involves analyzing financial statements, assessing market position, and often enlisting the help of a professional appraiser. This valuation not only informs the asking price but also provides a justified basis for negotiation with potential buyers.

Enhancing Attractiveness

Enhancing the attractiveness of your LLC to potential buyers is another crucial step. This may include:

- **Streamlining Operations**: Optimize management practices and operational efficiency to demonstrate a well-run business.

- **Improving Financial Metrics**: Focus on enhancing cash flow and profit margins, which can make your business more appealing.

- **Addressing Outstanding Issues**: Resolve any legal matters, outdated systems, or other issues that could detract from the business's value.

These improvements can significantly increase your business's market value and make it more appealing to potential buyers.

Streamlining Documentation

Ensuring that all aspects of your business are running efficiently is vital. This includes organizing and updating documentation, such as contracts, financial records, and client lists. Having these documents in order not only attracts buyers but also smooths the due diligence process, potentially speeding up the sale.

Marketing the Business for Sale

Finding the right buyer for your LLC requires proactive marketing strategies rather than simply waiting for offers to come in. **Employing a Business Broker** can be advantageous in this phase. Brokers have networks of potential buyers and extensive experience in negotiating business sales, making them invaluable allies. They can manage much of the marketing and initial screening of potential buyers, allowing you to focus on running your business during the sale process.

Online Business-for-Sale Marketplaces are another effective tool. These platforms can reach a wide audience of potential buyers, including those who may not be in your immediate geographic area but are actively looking for opportunities like yours. When listing your business, be sure to highlight its strengths and growth potential while being transparent about any challenges. Transparency can help build trust with potential buyers.

Leveraging Industry Contacts can also be a powerful strategy. Networking within your industry can reveal potential buyers who already understand the market and see immediate value in your business. Attend industry conferences, engage with professional associations, or pursue direct outreach to create connections that can lead to opportunities not available through more general marketing channels.

Negotiating the Sale

Negotiation is where your preparation and marketing efforts converge to realize the financial and strategic value of your business. Understanding the motivations of potential buyers is key to effective negotiations. Some buyers may be interested in a strategic acquisition that complements their existing businesses, while others might be attracted by your company's standalone profitability or growth potential. Tailoring your negotiation tactics based on the buyer's motivations can lead to mutually beneficial deals.

Common deal structures in selling an LLC include **asset sales**, where the buyer purchases the business assets outright, and **stock sales**, where the buyer acquires the ownership interests of the company. Each structure has different tax and liability implications, so choosing the right one can impact both the immediate financial outcomes and the long-term success of the transaction.

During negotiations, consider the **terms of payment**—whether the buyer will pay all cash upfront or if seller financing will be part of the deal. Seller financing, where you act as a lender, can make your business more attractive to buyers who may lack sufficient capital or credit to secure traditional financing. However, this approach also means you assume the risk if the new owner fails to make the business profitable.

Handling the Transition

A smooth transition is crucial for preserving the value of the business you've built and ensuring its ongoing success under new ownership. This phase involves transferring knowledge, processes, and relationships to the new owner. Agreeing to stay on in a consultancy role for a period after the sale can ease the transition and provide the new owner with valuable insights and experience that help maintain business continuity.

Additionally, addressing any **post-sale liabilities**, such as employee contracts, existing customer agreements, or lease arrangements, is essential. Ensuring these obligations are clearly outlined and understood by the new owner can prevent legal complications and help maintain operational stability.

Selling your LLC is a significant milestone, and approaching it with a strategic mindset can lead to a more favorable outcome, ensuring you receive fair value for your investment and that the business continues to thrive. As you prepare to embark on new ventures or enjoy the rewards of your hard work, the satisfaction of a well-executed sale can be a profound source of pride and closure.

As we wrap up this exploration of advanced financial management strategies, remember that successful financial oversight involves not only understanding the intricate details of financial operations, tax strategies, and funding options but also preparing for eventual transitions—whether through growth, restructuring, or sale. The insights and strategies discussed here equip you with the knowledge to navigate these complex processes, ensuring your business's financial health and aligning with your long-term goals.

In the next chapter, we will delve into the legal nuances of running an LLC, providing a comprehensive guide to legal compliance, risk management, and intellectual property protection—further ensuring your business's success and longevity.

CHAPTER

SEVEN

Navigating Challenges

Overcoming Common Entrepreneurial Obstacles

As you steer your LLC toward success, the road inevitably presents various hurdles—some anticipated, others catching you off guard. These challenges can either forge your business into a resilient entity or, if not navigated wisely, become stumbling blocks to your growth. This chapter equips you with savvy strategies and practical insights to not only face these obstacles but leverage them to your advantage, ensuring your business thrives in the dynamic landscape of entrepreneurship.

Identifying Typical Obstacles

In the life of an entrepreneur, certain challenges recur with enough frequency that they become almost a rite of passage. Cash flow concerns, the quest for talent retention, and the complexities inherent in managing growth are just a few of the common hurdles every business owner must clear.

Cash Flow Challenges

Cash flow issues often top the list of challenges. Cash flow is the lifeblood of your business, and when it runs dry, the entire operation can grind to a halt. Whether clients delay payments, unexpected expenses arise, or seasonal dips in revenue occur, maintaining healthy cash flow requires diligent oversight and proactive management.

Talent Acquisition and Retention

Finding and retaining top talent is another significant challenge. Your team is the driving force behind your LLC, a source of innovation and growth. However, in today's competitive job market, attracting the right candidates and keeping them motivated and committed can be daunting.

Managing Growth

Managing growth, particularly rapid growth, presents its own set of challenges. Scaling your business isn't just about increasing sales; it involves enlarging your operational capacity, managing larger teams, and maintaining the quality of your product or service amidst the strain of expansion.

Strategies to Overcome Financial Hurdles

To navigate cash flow fluctuations, start by establishing robust invoicing and follow-up procedures to ensure timely payments from clients. Consider offering incentives for early payment and penalties for late payments to encourage quicker turnover. Additionally, diversifying your revenue streams can buffer your business against financial dips; if one product line underperforms, another might fill the gap.

Exploring alternative financing options can provide a lifeline when conventional funding isn't sufficient or forthcoming. From lines of credit to invoice financing and angel investments, understanding the spectrum of available financial solutions enables you to make informed decisions that stabilize your business's finances.

Implementing cost-cutting measures can also help navigate financial straits. This doesn't necessarily mean slashing your workforce or skimping on essential services. Instead, analyze your expenses critically to identify areas where efficiencies can be gained—renegotiating vendor contracts, reducing unnecessary subscriptions, or implementing energy-saving measures.

Maintaining Employee Morale and Retention

Creating a positive work environment significantly enhances employee retention. This encompasses not only the physical workspace but also the cultural and emotional aspects of the workplace. Recognizing and rewarding efforts and achievements can boost morale and foster a sense of loyalty and belonging among your team.

Investing in Employee Development

Investing in employee development is crucial for fostering a committed and capable team. Offering training programs, opportunities for career advancement, and regular feedback sessions helps employees feel valued and invested in your business's future. Additionally, ensure that your leadership style is inclusive and supportive, promoting open communication and collaboration. This approach enhances team cohesion and productivity, ultimately benefiting the entire organization.

Adapting to Rapid Growth

To effectively manage the challenges of rapid growth, begin by ensuring your operational processes and infrastructure can scale accordingly. This may involve adopting more sophisticated project management software, expanding your facilities, or hiring additional staff to handle increased demand.

Quality Control

Quality control is paramount as you scale. Implement regular reviews and quality checks to ensure that your product or service remains consistent as your business grows. This practice not only maintains your brand's reputation but also keeps your customers satisfied.

Agility and Market Responsiveness

Staying agile and responsive to market demands is crucial during periods of expansion. Pay close attention to customer feedback and be prepared to pivot or make adjustments to your offerings in response to consumer needs and industry trends. By approaching these common entrepreneurial challenges with a strategic mindset and practical solutions, you can navigate your business through turbulent times with confidence. This proactive and prepared approach strengthens your business against immediate obstacles and lays a robust foundation for sustainable growth and success.

Dealing with Seasonal Fluctuations in Business

For many businesses, seasonal fluctuations are a fact of life—an ebb and flow that can dictate the pace and profitability of operations. Whether it's an ice cream shop facing a downturn in winter or a ski equipment retailer experiencing slow summer months, understanding how to anticipate and plan for these changes is crucial.

Analyzing Sales Data

Start with a thorough analysis of your past sales data and market trends. From this data, you can predict the ups and downs your business might see in the coming year. This analysis isn't just about bracing for slow periods; it's about strategically leveraging busy times as well. Adjust your budget to accommodate anticipated income fluctuations by increasing your marketing spend during peak seasons to maximize revenue, while possibly lowering it during off-peak times and focusing on cost-saving measures.

Resource Allocation

Resource allocation during these fluctuations is equally important. If your business requires additional staff during the holiday season, plan for this by hiring temporary workers. This strategy meets short-term needs while avoiding the expense and complication of laying off permanent staff when business slows. Effectively managing inventory ensures you don't find yourself with excess stock when demand wanes;

implementing just-in-time inventory systems can help you order stock in line with demand, significantly reducing holding costs and minimizing wastage.

Diversifying Offerings

Diversifying your product or service offerings can provide a buffer against seasonal dips. For example, a landscaping company might handle lawn care in the summer and offer snow removal in the winter. This strategy stabilizes income throughout the year and keeps staff employed, which helps maintain morale and reduce turnover. Consider offering holiday specials or off-season discounts to attract customers during slow periods or bundling services in unique ways that appeal to different customer segments.

Tailored Marketing Strategies

For businesses facing substantial off-season periods, effective marketing strategies tailored to these times can be a game-changer. Targeted advertising campaigns can reach specific demographics likely to purchase during off-peak times, with social media platforms enabling detailed targeting and immediate feedback. Hosting events or creating occasions, such as a "Christmas in July" sale, can generate buzz and attract customers during traditionally slow periods. Additionally, leveraging email marketing to offer special promotions or exclusive access to new products keeps your business on customers' minds year-round.

Developing a Crisis Management Plan

In the unpredictable world of business, crises are not a matter of if, but when. Having a well-defined crisis management plan is essential—not only for mitigating immediate damage but also for preserving your reputation and ensuring the longevity of your LLC. Think of this plan as your emergency blueprint, outlining precise steps to be taken when faced with a crisis. The key components of an effective crisis management plan include detailed communication strategies, clearly defined roles and responsibilities for your team, and structured recovery steps to guide your business back to normalcy.

Key Components of a Crisis Management Plan

1. Communication Strategy

A robust communication strategy is at the heart of any crisis management plan. This should detail how you will communicate with all stakeholders, including employees, customers, investors, and the media. Maintaining transparency during a crisis is crucial; provide regular updates as more information becomes available and as situations evolve. Additionally, include templates for press releases, social media responses, and internal communications to ensure consistency and clarity in your messages.

2. Roles and Responsibilities

Assigning roles and responsibilities is another critical element. Each team member should know their specific role in a crisis situation—whether it's managing customer inquiries, updating social media, or liaising with external crisis management teams. Regular training sessions and drills can help cement these roles, ensuring everyone knows what to do without hesitation. Include contact lists and any necessary access codes or passwords in the plan, enabling team members to perform their duties without delays.

3. Recovery Steps

Recovery steps must be clearly outlined. These are your roadmap for navigating out of the crisis and should include both short-term actions to stop the immediate crisis and longer-term strategies to recover any lost business or repair damage to your reputation. This might involve reviewing and strengthening your business's operational areas that failed, addressing vulnerabilities, and implementing stronger safeguards to prevent future crises.

Handling Immediate Crisis Responses

When a crisis strikes, the initial response can set the tone for how the situation unfolds. It's crucial that these first actions are swift, coordinated, and effective. Begin by assembling your crisis management team immediately to assess the situation and activate your crisis management plan. This team should have the authority to make crucial decisions quickly and access all areas of your business to gather accurate information about the crisis.

1. Effective Communication with Stakeholders

Communication with stakeholders is paramount in these early stages. Start by informing internal teams to ensure that all employees understand the situation and their roles in managing it. Misinformation can spread quickly, so providing clear and accurate updates is essential to maintain trust and control over the narrative. When communicating with external stakeholders, such as customers and the public, ensure the information is consistent across all channels. This might involve updating your business website, issuing press releases, and posting on social and professional networks.

2. Managing Media Relations

Managing media relations is another crucial aspect of your initial response. Designate a single spokesperson to handle all media inquiries, ensuring a unified and consistent message. Prepare this spokesperson with key messages and anticipated questions to maintain composure and professionalism during interviews or press conferences. This helps control the narrative and mitigate potential damage to your business's reputation.

3. Mitigating Damage

Finally, take actionable steps to address the root cause of the crisis. This may involve halting certain operations, issuing recalls if your business deals with physical products, or implementing security measures in case of a data breach.

Learning from Crisis Situations

Once a crisis has been navigated, the work isn't over. The post-crisis phase is crucial for fortifying your business against future challenges. Begin with a detailed analysis of what went wrong and what was handled well. Involve key members of your crisis management team in this review and encourage them to provide honest feedback about the response efforts. This analysis should cover all aspects of the crisis, including how it was initially detected, the effectiveness of internal and external communication, and the efficiency of the recovery steps.

Documenting Insights

Documenting these insights is essential. Develop a comprehensive report that outlines the sequence of events during the crisis, evaluates the effectiveness of your crisis management plan, and notes areas for improvement. This document should serve as a learning tool and a basis for updating your crisis management plan.

Implementing Lessons Learned

Implement the lessons learned by updating your crisis management strategies. This may involve additional training for your team, revising communication protocols, or enhancing your monitoring systems to detect potential crises earlier. Regularly revisiting and practicing the updated plan is crucial to ensure everyone remains prepared and confident in their ability to handle future crises.

Building Resilience in Business Operations

Building resilience in your business operations is key to surviving future crises. This involves several strategies that fortify your business from the inside out.

1. Diversifying Your Supply Chain

Diversifying your supply chain is one effective strategy. Relying on a single supplier or region can leave your business vulnerable to disruptions. By establishing relationships with multiple suppliers across different regions, you can ensure that a disruption in one area doesn't halt your entire operation.

2. Investing in Risk Management

Investing in comprehensive risk management is another crucial strategy. Conduct regular risk assessments to identify potential vulnerabilities in your operations, finances, or cybersecurity. Based on these assessments, implement appropriate measures to mitigate risks, such as purchasing insurance, establishing robust cybersecurity protocols, and creating emergency funds to cover unexpected financial needs.

3. Maintaining Strong Liquidity

Maintaining strong liquidity is also essential for building operational resilience. Ensure your business has access to sufficient cash reserves or liquid assets that can be quickly mobilized in a crisis. This financial cushion can be the difference between weathering a storm and closing your doors. Regular financial reviews and prudent financial management practices can help maintain the necessary liquidity to support your business through uncertain times.

Renewing Your Business Model

In the dynamic realm of business, staying relevant means staying adaptable. Recognizing when your business model needs a refresh is crucial—not just for survival, but for thriving in an ever-changing marketplace. Signals indicating the need for this can include a noticeable decline in sales, shifts in market demands, or the emergence of new competitors that alter the playing field. For instance, a sudden drop in sales might not just reflect a temporary downturn; it could indicate that your customers' needs have evolved beyond what your current offerings provide. Likewise, new competitors can introduce innovative business models or technologies that disrupt the market, forcing you to rethink your strategies to maintain your competitive edge.

Adopting Innovative Business Models

To stay ahead, consider adopting innovative business models that have reshaped entire industries. Subscription services, for example, have transformed everything from software (SaaS models like Adobe Creative Cloud) to consumer goods (services like Dollar Shave Club). These models attract customers with the promise of convenience and value, offering consistent revenue streams for businesses. Similarly, the freemium strategy—used by companies like Spotify and LinkedIn— provides a basic service for free with the option to upgrade for premium features. This approach can rapidly expand your user base, with monetization focused on a smaller segment that opts for paid features. Additionally, platform-based businesses like Airbnb and Uber have revolutionized their respective industries by facilitating exchanges between users and service providers, leveraging scalable technology to create value through community-driven marketplaces.

Implementing Change Gradually

When introducing changes to your business model, start small to minimize risks. Test new ideas through pilot projects or limited releases to gather actionable feedback without overcommitting resources. This approach allows you to evaluate how a new model performs in a controlled environment and make necessary adjustments before rolling it out fully. For example, if considering a subscription model, you might initially offer it to a select group of loyal and engaged customers. Their feedback will provide invaluable insights, helping you fine-tune the model based on real user experiences before expanding it to your broader market.

Tracking Success and Adjusting

Monitoring and adjusting the new model is an ongoing process that requires attention to detail and an openness to continual learning. Utilize key performance indicators (KPIs) relevant to the new business model to track its effectiveness. Metrics such as **customer acquisition cost**, **customer lifetime value**, **churn rate**, and **revenue growth** are critical in assessing the health and viability of your model. Regularly review these metrics and gather customer feedback to stay informed about your business's performance. If certain aspects of the new model underperform or market conditions shift, be prepared to iterate and refine your approach. This agility often distinguishes successful businesses that adapt and thrive from those that stagnate.

By embracing innovation and being willing to transform your business model in response to market signals, you position your business not only to respond to changes but to lead them. This proactive approach ensures your business remains relevant, responsive, and resilient, no matter what challenges the market brings.

Learning from Competitive Analysis

Understanding your competitors goes beyond tracking their actions; it's about deeply analyzing their strategies to refine your own. Conducting an effective competitive analysis involves several steps that offer a clearer view of the landscape in which your LLC operates.

Start by identifying your key competitors, including direct competitors offering similar products or services, and indirect competitors whose offerings might substitute or overlap with yours. Use tools like industry reports, customer feedback, and social media monitoring to gather data.

Next, assess their strengths and weaknesses. What are they excelling at? Where are they falling short? Evaluate factors like product quality, customer service, marketing, and pricing. This assessment provides a benchmark for your business. For example, if a competitor excels in customer service but charges higher prices, you may find an opportunity to attract price-conscious customers who still value good service. This analysis helps identify gaps not only in their strategies but in your own as well.

Then, analyze their marketing strategies. What channels are they using? How are they positioning themselves in the market? What customer segments are they targeting? Understanding these elements offers insights into their business priorities, helping you anticipate their next moves. If a competitor invests heavily in digital marketing, it could indicate a focus on younger, tech-savvy consumers, suggesting shifts in market dynamics that may influence your strategies.

Gaining Insights from Competitor Successes and Failures

Learning from your competitors' successes and failures provides invaluable lessons. Analyze specific campaigns or product launches that either thrived or faltered. What contributed to their success or downfall? These insights are especially useful when expanding into new markets or product lines. For instance, if a competitor's expansion failed due to inadequate market research, it serves as a reminder to conduct thorough analysis before scaling your operations.

These case studies not only offer lessons but also inspire innovation. They foster a mindset focused on continuous improvement and differentiation. By taking a proactive approach, your business stays aligned with market trends and often sets them, keeping your operations dynamic and forward-thinking.

Gaining Insights from Competitor Successes and Failures

Learning from both the successes and failures of your competitors is invaluable. Each scenario provides a roadmap for what to emulate or avoid. Conducting case studies on specific campaigns or product launches—whether they succeeded or failed—can offer useful insights. For instance, if a competitor's rapid expansion failed due to insufficient market research, it's a reminder to prioritize thorough market analysis before venturing into new territories.

These case studies not only serve as lessons but also inspire innovation within your own business. This proactive approach allows your business to not just keep pace with market trends but to set them, keeping your operations dynamic, competitive, and forward-thinking.

Adapting Strategies Based on Analysis

The true value of competitive analysis lies in how you use the insights to enhance your own strategies. If your analysis reveals unmet customer needs among competitors, consider how your business could address these gaps. This might involve tweaking your product offerings, adjusting pricing, or improving customer service. Similarly, if competitors are successfully using certain marketing strategies, evaluate how these tactics can be adapted to fit your business. For example, incorporating more digital marketing techniques or leveraging social media could enhance your visibility and customer engagement.

Moreover, competitive analysis should be an ongoing process, not a one-time task. The business landscape is constantly evolving, and keeping track of your competitors' actions ensures you stay competitive. Establish a system for regular reviews—monthly or quarterly—to assess changes in your competitors' strategies, market position, or customer base. This continuous monitoring enables your business to remain agile and quickly respond to shifts in the competitive landscape.

By incorporating insights from competitive analysis into your business strategy, you can mitigate risks and seize opportunities that might have otherwise been overlooked. This approach not only enhances your operational effectiveness but also drives sustained growth and success.

Looking ahead, these insights form an integral part of your business's strategic planning. They help shape a responsive and proactive business model that addresses current market needs while anticipating future trends. This preparation enables your business not just to react to the market but to actively shape it, ensuring long-term relevance in a competitive environment.

As we transition from understanding competitive landscapes to exploring strategies for customer loyalty and retention in the next chapter, remember that continuous learning and adaptation are at the heart of gaining a competitive advantage.

CHAPTER

EIGHT

Special Topics in LLC Management

Navigating the Digital Marketplace

Exploring the burgeoning digital marketplace can be as thrilling as it is daunting. As you consider integrating e-commerce into your LLC, it's like embarking on a journey across vast digital oceans filled with boundless opportunities. However, without a well-charted plan and a solid foundation, you could easily veer off course. This chapter will serve as your compass, guiding you through the complexities of online sales—from setting up an e-commerce platform to mastering legal requirements and optimizing digital marketing strategies. By the end, your LLC will be well-equipped to navigate the competitive waters of e-commerce and reach lucrative markets.

E-commerce and Your LLC

Setting Up an E-commerce Platform

The first step in your e-commerce journey is selecting the right platform, which forms the backbone of your online business operations. This decision is crucial, as it impacts everything from your website's functionality to the overall user experience. Platforms like Shopify, Magento, and WooCommerce offer various features tailored to different business sizes and needs. For example, Shopify provides an easy-to-use interface with integrated payment solutions, ideal for newcomers, while Magento offers extensive customization options for more tech-savvy users with specific requirements.

Integrating reliable payment gateways is also essential. These gateways are how revenue flows into your business, so ensuring their security and efficiency is critical. Popular options like PayPal, Stripe, and Square are known for their strong security measures and wide acceptance. However, it's important to select gateways that align with your customers' preferences and geographic location to provide a seamless checkout experience.

Additionally, security compliance is paramount. Ensuring your platform meets PCI DSS standards (Payment Card Industry Data Security Standard) protects against breaches and fosters customer trust. Implementing SSL certificates to encrypt data and conducting regular security audits will further protect your e-commerce platform, ensuring customer transactions are safe from cyber threats.

Legal Considerations for Online Sales

As you delve into e-commerce, understanding and adhering to legal requirements is essential for maintaining the integrity and legality of your online operations. Key considerations include privacy policies, data protection regulations, and consumer rights. Crafting a clear, comprehensive privacy policy that outlines how customer data is collected, used, and protected isn't just a legal requirement—it's fundamental to building consumer trust.

Compliance with data protection laws, such as GDPR in Europe or CCPA in California, requires careful attention to how customer data is handled and stored. These regulations mandate that businesses implement strict measures to protect personal information and provide transparency about users' data rights. Non-compliance can result in hefty fines and significant damage to your business's reputation, so consulting legal professionals or using specialized compliance services is strongly recommended.

Understanding Consumer Protection Laws

Understanding consumer protection laws governing online sales is essential. These laws ensure that customers receive fair treatment and accurate information about the products or services they purchase online. This includes transparency in pricing, the right to cancel orders within a specific period, and clear return and refund policies. Adhering to these regulations not only ensures legal compliance but also boosts customer satisfaction and loyalty.

Optimizing Online Marketing Strategies

In the digital marketplace, your marketing strategies must be dynamic and adaptable. Search Engine Optimization (SEO) ensures that your products appear prominently in search engine results, driving organic traffic to your website. This involves optimizing content with relevant keywords, improving loading speeds, and securing quality backlinks.

Pay-Per-Click (PPC) advertising on platforms like Google Ads and Bing Ads allows you to place your products directly in front of potential customers actively searching for related items. Effective PPC requires careful keyword research and ongoing campaign adjustments to maximize your return on investment (ROI).

Email marketing remains one of the most effective ways to engage with customers. Segmenting your email list based on customer behavior and preferences enables personalized communication, which promotes higher engagement. Tools like Mailchimp and Campaign Monitor provide robust solutions for managing targeted email campaigns.

Social media platforms like Facebook, Instagram, and Pinterest offer powerful avenues for promoting products through targeted ads and engaging content. These platforms allow direct interaction with customers, helping you build a community around your brand while driving both sales and brand awareness.

Handling Logistics and Fulfillment

A strong logistics and fulfillment strategy is the backbone of successful e-commerce. This includes everything from inventory management to shipping logistics and handling returns. Implementing an efficient inventory management system allows you to track stock levels in real time, forecast demand, and replenish stock efficiently. This minimizes the risk of overstocking or running out of products, ensuring that your capital isn't tied up in unsold inventory and that customers receive their orders promptly.

Choosing the Right Shipping Solutions

Selecting the appropriate shipping solutions is crucial for ensuring timely, cost-effective deliveries. Whether you handle shipping in-house or partner with third-party logistics providers, the goal is to offer a reliable delivery experience. Consider providing multiple shipping options, such as standard, expedited, and same-day delivery, to accommodate different customer needs and preferences.

A clear and concise return policy is equally important for customer satisfaction. This policy should detail how customers can return products, the timeframe for returns, and any conditions that apply. Streamlining this process encourages customer trust and repeat business, transforming one-time buyers into loyal customers.

By carefully establishing your e-commerce platform with the right tools and strategies, adhering to legal requirements, optimizing marketing efforts, and managing logistics and fulfillment effectively, your LLC can not only survive but thrive in the competitive digital marketplace. Each step, though challenging, lays the groundwork for your business to expand its reach, increase sales, and build a strong online presence.

International Trade Considerations

As your LLC ventures into international markets, the complexity of operations grows, but so do the opportunities for expansion and diversification. Engaging in international trade requires a thorough understanding of export and import regulations, which are vital for navigating the global marketplace. Every country enforces specific trade rules, including tariffs—taxes imposed on imported goods and services. These tariffs can significantly impact your product pricing, making it essential to factor them into your pricing strategy.

Securing the necessary export licenses is a critical step in legally exporting goods. These licenses ensure that your business complies with national security and foreign policy regulations, with requirements varying based on the product or service and its destination. For example, technology products with potential military applications may require additional scrutiny before an export license is granted. Navigating these intricacies often requires consulting trade experts or legal advisors specializing in international commerce.

Customs procedures also play a pivotal role in international trade. These procedures involve submitting detailed documentation about your products—such as their value, quantity, and nature—to facilitate their legal entry into a foreign country. Missteps in customs documentation can lead to delays, penalties, or even the seizure of goods, which could disrupt operations and harm your business's reputation. Therefore, ensuring accurate and complete customs documentation, along with an understanding of each country's legal requirements, is vital for smooth international operations.

Navigating Cultural and Market Differences in International Trade

Navigating cultural and market differences is essential in international trade. Cultural nuances significantly influence consumer behavior, meaning that strategies effective in one country may not resonate in another. For example, direct and assertive sales tactics may be welcomed in some Western cultures but could be perceived as offensive in regions where business interactions are expected to be more subtle and relationship-focused. Understanding and respecting local business practices and holidays is equally crucial; scheduling a meeting during a major local festival can be seen as insensitive and may harm business relationships.

Adapting Communication Styles

Communication styles must also align with the cultural context of the target market. In high-context cultures, much is conveyed through implicit messages and non-verbal cues, while low-context cultures favor explicit and direct communication. Adapting your communication style to fit the cultural context can facilitate smoother interactions and negotiations, enhancing your business's ability to operate effectively in international markets.

Securing International Payments

Securing efficient and secure international payment methods is paramount for managing financial transactions. Traditional methods like letters of credit provide high security by involving banks from both the exporter's and importer's sides to ensure that payment terms are strictly followed before any funds are transferred. This approach significantly reduces the risk of non-payment, offering assurance to both parties.

Electronic funds transfer is another popular option, allowing quick and direct transactions. However, it requires a good understanding of exchange rates and transaction fees to ensure you receive the correct amount for your goods or services. Given the complexities of international payments, relying on experienced payment processors can help mitigate risks such as currency fluctuations and non-compliance with foreign financial regulations.

Building International Relationships

Building and maintaining international business relationships is another cornerstone of successful international trade. These relationships extend beyond customers to include partners, suppliers, and local market influencers. Networking is vital in this regard; attending industry conferences, trade shows, and international business meetings can provide valuable contacts and insights into the latest market trends. Effective networking involves not just exchanging information but also fostering trust and mutual respect, which are crucial for establishing long-term business relationships.

Understanding Negotiation Tactics

Negotiation tactics vary widely across cultures. In some cultures, negotiations are swift and to the point, while in others, they involve a lengthy process of building relationships and trust before discussing business terms. Understanding these differences and adapting your negotiation strategies accordingly can significantly enhance your chances of securing favorable deals. Being well-prepared, respecting local customs, and demonstrating a genuine interest in fostering mutually beneficial relationships contribute greatly to successful international negotiations.

By mastering these critical aspects of international trade—regulatory compliance, cultural adaptations, securing payments, and building robust business relationships—your LLC can effectively expand its operations globally. This strategic approach not only enhances your business's growth potential but also strengthens its resilience against domestic market fluctuations, laying a solid foundation for sustained success in the global marketplace.

Franchising Your Business

When considering the expansion of your LLC, franchising can be a transformative strategy for both growth and brand proliferation. This model allows others to operate under your established business name, systems, and processes, leading to rapid expansion and increased brand presence. However, not every business is suited for this growth path. In this section, we will evaluate your business's potential for franchising, develop a comprehensive franchising plan, understand franchise laws, and perfect strategies to attract franchisees.

Assessing Your Business Model for Franchising

The first step in this journey is determining whether your business model is suitable for franchising. Key factors play a pivotal role in this evaluation:

Uniqueness of Your Brand: Does your business offer something distinctive that is difficult for others to replicate? This could range from a unique product or service to an innovative business method or marketing strategy. The strength and appeal of your brand are vital, as these are what potential franchisees will invest in.

Profitability: For a franchise to be attractive, it must demonstrate proven profitability, reassuring potential franchisees of its viability and success potential.

Replicability: Is your business model easy to replicate? Your operations, training, and marketing strategies should be teachable to new franchise owners who will implement them across diverse markets.

Developing a Comprehensive Franchising Plan

A franchising plan serves as your blueprint for managing and supporting your franchise system. This plan should include:

Operational Guidelines: Detailed descriptions of your business model, including branding strategies and financial management.

Training Programs: Comprehensive training for franchisees covering day-to-day operations, staff management, local marketing, and compliance with regulatory requirements.

Legal Agreements: Drafting detailed legal agreements to govern relationships with franchisees. These agreements should clearly outline the terms of the franchise, including the rights and obligations of both the franchisor and franchisees, the franchise duration, renewal provisions, and terms regarding the use of intellectual property.

Navigating the Legal Landscape of Franchising

Navigating the legal landscape of franchising is crucial. Various laws regulate the franchising sector to protect both franchisors and franchisees. One key legal requirement is the Franchise Disclosure Document (FDD), which must be provided to potential franchisees. This document offers a comprehensive overview of the franchise, including the history of the franchisor, a detailed breakdown of financial expectations, and any legal obligations.

Additionally, franchise laws govern marketing practices to ensure that promotional materials and sales tactics are fair and transparent. These laws can vary by region, making it essential to understand the specific requirements in the areas where you plan to offer franchises. Consulting with a lawyer specializing in franchise law is advisable to navigate these regulations effectively and ensure compliance in your franchising efforts.

Marketing Your Franchise

Marketing your franchise is the final piece of the puzzle. Effective marketing strategies not only attract potential franchisees but also establish your franchise's credibility. Participating in franchise expos is a proven method, providing a platform to showcase your business to a large audience of potential franchisees. These events facilitate direct interaction, allowing you to present your business model, discuss the benefits of your franchise, and build relationships with potential investors.

Digital marketing strategies, such as targeted advertising campaigns, search engine optimization (SEO), and content marketing, are also essential. These online tactics enhance visibility and attract potential franchisees who are searching for franchising opportunities. Additionally, direct outreach through industry contacts, franchising consultants, and business networks can be highly effective. This personalized approach leverages existing relationships to promote your franchising opportunities.

By carefully evaluating your business's suitability for franchising, meticulously planning your franchising strategy, understanding and complying with franchise laws, and implementing effective marketing tactics, you can successfully expand your business through franchising. This multi-faceted approach not only facilitates growth but also enhances your brand's market presence, laying a robust foundation for long-term success in a competitive business landscape.

Innovations in Your Industry and Their Impacts

In the fast-paced world of business, staying current with industry trends is essential for strategically leveraging advancements to propel your LLC forward. Innovations—whether technological breakthroughs or shifts in consumer behavior—can drastically alter the competitive landscape. Engaging actively with your industry through trade shows, professional associations, and authoritative publications is vital.

Trade shows serve not only as networking venues but also as fertile grounds for witnessing firsthand emerging technologies and consumer trends that could shape your sector. Professional associations offer a wealth of resources, including specialized research, expert panels, and case studies, which can deepen your understanding of how certain innovations impact your industry. Staying informed through respected publications can provide ongoing insights and forecasts crucial for strategic planning.

Assessing the Impact of New Technologies on Your Business

Assessing the impact of new technologies on your business operations and market position requires a structured approach. Begin by identifying technologies that are gaining traction in your industry. For example, in the retail sector, augmented reality (AR) is transforming how consumers interact with products online. Evaluate how such technologies could enhance or disrupt your business processes, customer experiences, or value propositions. It's essential to consider both the opportunities and threats these innovations present. Conduct a SWOAT analysis (Strengths, Weaknesses, Opportunities, and Threats augmented by Technological insights) to systematically assess their potential impacts. This analysis will help you understand the implications of adopting these technologies and prepare for any competitive disruptions they might cause.

Incorporating Innovation into Your Business Strategy

Incorporating innovation into your business strategy is about embedding it into the DNA of your LLC, not just adopting new technologies. Consider allocating resources for research and development (R&D) to innovate from within. Additionally, partnerships with tech companies can provide access to cutting-edge technologies and expertise that may be too costly or complex to develop independently. Launching pilot projects to test new technologies or business models on a smaller scale before full implementation allows you to assess effectiveness and fine-tune execution in a controlled environment, minimizing potential risks and resource expenditures.

Building a Culture of Flexibility and Continuous Learning

Preparing your business to adapt to potential disruptions from technological advancements requires fostering a culture of flexibility and continuous learning within your team. Encourage employees to engage in ongoing learning through formal training programs and by promoting innovation and experimentation. This empowerment enables your team to adapt more quickly to changes, giving your business a competitive edge. Additionally, integrate flexible processes and IT systems that can be easily updated as new technologies emerge. This agility ensures you can capitalize on new opportunities without being hindered by outdated systems or rigid procedures.

Leveraging Industry Innovations for Growth

As you navigate the complexities of industry innovations, remember that the goal is not just to adapt but to leverage these changes for growth and competitive advantage. By staying informed, carefully assessing impacts, strategically integrating innovations, and proactively preparing for disruptions, your LLC can not only survive but thrive in an ever-evolving business landscape.

In wrapping up this chapter on special topics in LLC management, we have explored a variety of terrains—from leveraging e-commerce and understanding international trade to adopting sustainable practices and exploring franchising. Each of these areas presents unique opportunities and challenges, highlighting the importance of agility and foresight in effective business management. As we transition to the next chapter, we will delve deeper into strategies that will ensure your LLC not only meets but exceeds its operational and strategic goals.

CHAPTER
NINE

Building a Brand

Building a Brand: Crafting a Story That Resonates

Building a brand is akin to crafting a compelling story that resonates deeply with your audience—a narrative woven into every aspect of your business that distinguishes it in the bustling marketplace. Your brand is more than just a logo or color scheme; it embodies the emotional and psychological connection you cultivate with your customers. Once solidified, this connection becomes the lifeblood of your business, influencing how your products or services are perceived and, ultimately, how they perform in the market. Let's embark on refining your brand identity, ensuring it captures the essence of what you stand for while robustly positioning you against competitors and protecting the intellectual assets you create along the way.

Crafting a Strong Brand Identity

Defining Brand Elements

Your brand's visual elements—logo, color scheme, and typography—serve as the spearhead of your identity, acting as silent ambassadors for your brand. These elements should be meticulously chosen to reflect the core values and appeal of your business. Consider your logo, for instance; this pivotal graphic will appear on everything from your website and packaging to your business cards and marketing materials. It should be distinctive yet simple enough to be memorable. Engage a professional designer or use high-quality design tools to ensure that your logo makes a strong and lasting impression.

Equally important is your choice of color scheme. Colors possess the power to evoke emotions and set the tone for your brand. For example, blue may convey trust and dependability, while green often symbolizes growth and sustainability. Choose colors that not only complement each other but also help to tell your brand's story. Typography, the style of your text, plays a crucial role as well. The fonts you select should be legible across various mediums and resonate with your brand's character. Whether you opt for modern sans-serif fonts or more traditional serif fonts, ensure consistency across all communications to maintain a cohesive brand image.

Brand Messaging Consistency

Consistency is the backbone of effective branding. It ensures that every interaction customers have with your brand reinforces their perception of who you are. Your brand message should permeate every piece of content you create—from your website copy and marketing materials to your social media posts and customer service. A consistent voice and tone reassure customers of your brand's stability and reliability, fostering trust over time.

To achieve this consistency, develop a brand style guide that outlines how your brand should be presented across different platforms. This guide should include specifics on tone, language, and the overall messaging approach, serving as a reference point for anyone creating content for your brand.

Differentiation from Competitors

In a sea of competitors, your brand must stand out. This differentiation begins with a Unique Value Proposition (UVP)—a clear statement that articulates the benefits of your offer, how you meet your customers' needs, and what sets you apart from the competition. To pinpoint your UVP, analyze your competitors' strengths and weaknesses, identifying gaps that your business can fill. Highlight these differences in your marketing campaigns, product development, and customer interactions. Whether it's superior customer service, innovative product features, or a unique selling point like sustainability, ensure these differentiators are visible and compelling to your target audience.

Legal Protection of Brand Assets

As your brand grows, protecting its intellectual property becomes paramount. Trademarks and copyrights are essential tools that safeguard your logo, name, taglines, and other brand elements from unauthorized use. Registering a trademark grants you exclusive rights to your brand elements, preventing others from using a similar identity that could confuse customers and dilute your brand's strength. Start this process by searching the U.S. Patent and Trademark Office's database to ensure your brand elements are unique, then file for protection under the categories that most closely align with your business activities. The benefits of this legal protection include the authority to enforce your rights in court, deterring potential infringements and providing a competitive edge in the marketplace.

By thoroughly defining and consistently promoting your brand elements, maintaining a coherent message, differentiating from competitors, and legally protecting your brand assets, you establish a strong brand identity that resonates with customers and stands the test of time. This identity not only fosters recognition and loyalty but also adds intrinsic value to your business, paving the way for sustained success and growth. As we continue to explore other facets of building a robust brand in the subsequent sections, keep these foundational principles in mind—they are the keystones of your brand's architecture, supporting every effort you make to connect with your audience and expand your market presence.

Effective Public Relations Strategies

In orchestrating the narrative surrounding your brand, public relations (PR) plays a pivotal role in shaping perceptions and building enduring relationships with your audience. A well-crafted PR strategy amplifies your brand's message and fortifies its reputation, especially during times of scrutiny or crisis. Let's delve into how you can establish a proactive PR plan, navigate crises with poise, foster robust media relationships, and measure the impact of your efforts to ensure your PR initiatives are not just seen but felt.

Developing a PR Plan

The essence of a successful PR strategy lies in preparation and precision. Start by setting clear, attainable objectives. What do you want to achieve with your PR efforts? Are you looking to enhance brand visibility, improve public perception, or manage the fallout from a previous issue? Once your goals are established, identify the key messages that align with these objectives. These messages should resonate with your core values and speak directly to the needs and emotions of your target audience.

Next, choose the right media outlets. Not all platforms are suitable for every message or audience. Select channels that your target demographic frequents and trusts, whether it's industry-specific magazines, mainstream media, or online platforms. Crafting a timeline for your PR activities is also crucial. This helps synchronize your efforts with other marketing campaigns and business activities, ensuring a cohesive brand presence across all touchpoints.

Each phase of your PR plan should be meticulously scheduled, from the initial media outreach to follow-ups after a story is published. This timeline should be flexible enough to adapt to unexpected opportunities or challenges that may arise, allowing you to maintain momentum and responsiveness in a dynamic media landscape. By methodically planning your PR strategy, you not only set the stage for measurable success but also create a framework that can adapt and evolve with your business.

Crisis Management in PR

Handling a crisis effectively is perhaps the most rigorous test of your PR strategy. The key to successful crisis management lies in swift, transparent, and controlled communication. Start by publicly acknowledging the issue and taking responsibility, if appropriate. This approach helps maintain trust and credibility with your audience. Clearly communicate the steps being taken to address the situation and outline what changes will be made to prevent future occurrences.

Centralizing communication is crucial to avoid conflicting messages that can exacerbate the crisis. Designate a spokesperson or a team of spokespeople who are well-versed in the crisis response plan and capable of conveying empathy and confidence under pressure.

Maintaining a proactive stance during a crisis involves extensive monitoring of public perception and media coverage. This enables you to adjust your strategies in real-time, addressing misconceptions and reinforcing positive narratives. Regular updates should be provided to all stakeholders, including employees, customers, and the media, keeping them informed and engaged throughout the resolution process. Effective crisis management not only mitigates immediate damage but can also enhance your brand's resilience and deepen trust with your audience over the long term.

Leveraging Media Relationships

Building and maintaining strong relationships with media professionals is fundamental to the success of your PR efforts. Begin by identifying key journalists and influencers in your industry who share your audience's interests. Engage with them regularly, not just when you need coverage. Offer insights, provide exclusive data, or invite them to company events. This builds rapport and a sense of partnership, making them more likely to cover your stories.

When pitching your story, tailor your approach to each journalist's interests and coverage history. Make your pitches compelling and newsworthy, focusing on how the story benefits their readers or viewers. Be responsive to their inquiries, provide necessary resources such as high-quality images or expert quotes, and respect their deadlines. This professionalism not only increases your chances of getting coverage but also establishes your brand as a reliable and valuable source of information.

Measuring PR Success

To gauge the effectiveness of your PR initiatives, define key performance indicators (KPIs) that reflect your objectives. These might include measures such as the amount of media coverage, sentiment of that coverage, audience reach, and engagement levels. Tools like media monitoring services can provide comprehensive data on where and how your brand is being mentioned across various channels. Analyzing this data helps you understand the impact of your PR efforts and identify areas for improvement.

Additionally, consider direct feedback from your audience through social media interactions and customer inquiries. This qualitative data offers deeper insights into public perception and the emotional impact of your PR strategies. By continuously measuring and refining your approach based on these insights, you ensure that your public relations efforts contribute positively to your brand's growth and reputation, aligning with your overall business goals and fostering a strong, enduring connection with your audience.

Utilizing Social Media for Brand Growth

In today's digital age, social media is a vital tool for brand building and engagement, providing a platform where your brand can not only communicate but also engage in meaningful dialogue with your audience. The key to leveraging social media effectively lies in understanding which platforms best align with your brand's identity and the demographics of your target audience.

Each platform, whether it's Instagram, Twitter, LinkedIn, or Facebook, has its unique environment and user base. For example, Instagram is visually driven and tends to attract a younger demographic, making it ideal for brands with visually appealing products or services aimed at millennials and Gen Z. In contrast, LinkedIn caters to professionals seeking to expand their networks, making it perfect for B2B companies looking to establish thought leadership and connect with other businesses.

Selecting the right platforms involves a strategic analysis of where your target customers are most active and where your content is likely to resonate. For instance, if your brand sells DIY crafts, platforms like Pinterest and Instagram may be more beneficial due to their strong focus on visuals and high engagement from craft enthusiasts.

Conversely, if your focus is on professional consulting services, LinkedIn and Twitter might be more appropriate for sharing industry insights and networking. Understanding these nuances allows you to tailor your social media efforts to platforms that will most effectively support your business goals, ensuring your resources are invested in areas with the highest potential return.

Creating Engaging Content

Captivating your audience with compelling content is a crucial step in building your brand. The content you share should reflect your brand's voice while providing real value to your followers. This can take various forms, such as informative blog posts, engaging videos, or interactive live sessions that address your audience's interests and needs.

Video Content

Video content is particularly effective for increasing engagement rates. Tutorials, behind-the-scenes glimpses, and customer testimonials are all excellent formats that not only showcase your brand but also foster a deeper connection with your audience. These visual elements make your brand more relatable and amplify the impact of your messages.

Live Streaming

Live streaming is another powerful tool for real-time engagement. Platforms like Facebook Live and Instagram Live allow you to interact directly with your audience, answering questions and responding to comments on the spot. This immediate interaction cultivates a sense of community and trust around your brand.

User-Generated Content (UGC)

Encouraging user-generated content (UGC) can also be incredibly effective. When customers share their own stories or experiences with your products, it adds authenticity to your brand and leverages the power of social proof. Potential customers are more likely to trust and engage with brands endorsed by real people.

Social Media Advertising

Social media advertising can significantly amplify your reach and impact. With advanced targeting options on platforms like Facebook and LinkedIn, you can tailor your advertising efforts to reach specific demographics, geographic locations, and user behaviors. This ensures that your ads are seen by those most likely to be interested in your products or services.

Effective social media advertising requires a careful balance of compelling visuals, engaging copy, and strategic targeting. Budgeting for these ads should align with clear objectives, whether it's increasing brand awareness, driving traffic to your website, or converting leads into sales. Continuously testing and adjusting your ads helps optimize spending and enhance ROI.

Building an Interactive Community

The true power of social media lies not just in broadcasting your message but in fostering an interactive community. Monitoring and responding to social interactions is crucial. Regularly review comments, messages, and reviews, responding promptly and respectfully. This practice not only helps manage your brand's reputation but also builds strong relationships with your audience.

Positive interactions, especially when addressing customer concerns, can significantly enhance customer loyalty and advocacy for your brand. By prioritizing engagement and responsiveness, you cultivate a community that supports and champions your brand.

Transforming Social Media into Valuable Assets

By effectively managing key aspects of social media—choosing the right platforms, creating engaging content, leveraging advertising, and maintaining active interactions—you can transform your social media channels into valuable assets for brand growth. Each interaction presents an opportunity to reinforce your brand's values, gather customer insights, and build lasting relationships that drive business success. As you continue to explore and refine your social media strategies, remember that consistency and authenticity are essential for creating a loyal community and achieving your business objectives in the vibrant, ever-evolving digital landscape.

Community Engagement and Corporate Responsibility

The influence of a business extends beyond its operations into the heart of the community it serves. Engaging with your local community isn't just an act of goodwill; it's a strategic move that can significantly enhance your brand's reputation, foster customer loyalty, and drive sustainable business growth. When you invest time and resources into community initiatives, you're building a foundation of trust and shared values that resonate with your customers and stakeholders.

Sponsoring Local Events

One effective way to engage with your community is through sponsoring local events. Whether it's a charity run, school function, or arts festival, sponsorship increases your brand visibility while demonstrating your commitment to the community's well-being. These events provide a platform to showcase your products or services and connect with potential customers in a positive environment. The events you support reflect your brand's values, aligning your business with causes that matter to your customer base.

Volunteering

Organizing volunteer days for employees to contribute to local charities or community projects is another powerful strategy. Not only does this help those in need, but it also strengthens your team. It fosters pride and loyalty among employees, enhances morale, and promotes a positive workplace culture. Customers are more likely to support businesses that visibly make a difference, translating into increased loyalty and word-of-mouth promotion.

Partnerships with Local Organizations

Building partnerships with local organizations, such as non-profits, schools, or other businesses, can amplify your impact on community projects and broaden your network. Collaborating on initiatives allows you to pool resources, share expertise, and increase the reach of your efforts. These collaborations can take many forms, from co-hosting community events to launching joint marketing campaigns. Such partnerships not only address local issues but also create a support network that propels your business forward.

Case Studies

Consider a regional grocery chain that launched a program to donate unsold produce to local food banks. This initiative reduced waste and addressed community hunger, enhancing the brand's image as a responsible organization. The grocery chain saw increased customer loyalty and positive media coverage. Another example is a tech company that partnered with local universities to create internships and training programs, helping students gain valuable skills while tapping into a pool of potential employees. These case studies illustrate how integrating community engagement into your brand strategy yields substantial benefits, enhancing your corporate reputation and bottom line.

By embedding community engagement and corporate responsibility into your branding strategy, you transform your business into a force for good, creating value that extends beyond profits. This approach endears your brand to community members and consumers, laying a foundation for lasting business success characterized by strong relationships, a positive public image, and a loyal customer base. As you move forward, consider how your business can continue to make a positive impact socially and environmentally, strengthening your connection with the community and paving the way for a sustainable future.

Building a Lasting Corporate Culture

Corporate culture is a potent aspect of a business's identity, representing the values and practices that shape employee behavior and influence business outcomes. A robust corporate culture aligns with your brand values and molds an internal environment that directly affects team morale, productivity, and retention rates. At its core, it's about creating a work environment that aligns business goals with the professional and personal growth of employees.

Open Communication

The foundation of a strong corporate culture is open communication. Encouraging transparency fosters trust throughout the organization. This can be achieved through regular team meetings, open-door policies, and platforms for employees to voice their ideas or concerns without fear of retribution. Such practices enhance teamwork and contribute to an agile business environment where issues are quickly addressed, and innovations can flourish.

Promoting Work-Life Balance

Promoting work-life balance is crucial in cultivating a positive workplace environment. This balance may include flexible working hours, remote work options, or wellness programs that address physical and mental health. For instance, offering flexible hours can accommodate personal commitments, reducing stress and increasing job satisfaction. These practices show that the company values its employees' well-being, leading to increased loyalty and lower turnover rates.

Recognizing Employee Achievements

Recognizing and celebrating employee achievements is equally important. Formal recognition programs, performance bonuses, or simple public acknowledgment can significantly boost morale and motivation. Celebrating successes reinforces the message that every individual's contributions are valued, fostering belonging and pride in their work.

Aligning Corporate Culture with Brand Identity

Aligning your corporate culture with your brand identity ensures consistency that resonates internally and externally. If customer service excellence is a cornerstone of your brand, fostering a culture that prioritizes exceptional service and proactive problem-solving reinforces this identity. Employees become brand ambassadors, mirroring the brand's values in their actions and attitudes. This alignment enhances authenticity and strengthens the overall brand experience for customers.

Navigating Growth and Change

As your business grows, maintaining a cohesive culture can be challenging, especially during significant changes such as mergers, acquisitions, or rapid scaling. It's crucial to manage cultural integration thoughtfully during these times. Aligning differing corporate cultures, integrating new employees into existing teams, and communicating company values clearly can help maintain cultural integrity. Regular training sessions, team-building activities, and ongoing communication of company values and goals can ease transitions and reinforce culture.

By investing in a workplace environment that promotes open communication, work-life balance, and employee recognition, and ensuring that this environment reflects your brand identity, you lay the pillars for a corporate culture that attracts and retains top talent. This culture becomes a critical asset in driving sustainable growth and success, making your business not just a place to work but a community that people are proud to be part of.

In this exploration of building a lasting corporate culture, we've delved into how a strong, aligned, and adaptive culture is essential for a thriving business. It supports immediate business objectives and bolsters long-term goals, ensuring that as your business evolves, your team remains engaged and motivated, driving forward with shared purpose and vision. As we transition into the next chapter, we'll shift our focus from internal dynamics to the broader strategic frameworks that guide successful business operations, ensuring your business not only survives but thrives in competitive environments.

CHAPTER

TEN

Preparing for the Future

Navigating the Crossroads of Business Decisions

Imagine standing at a crossroads where each path represents a potential future for your business. The decisions you make today, informed by a deep understanding of market dynamics and competitive intelligence, will determine the direction and success of your entrepreneurial venture. This chapter equips you with the tools and insights necessary to navigate these choices with foresight and agility.

Anticipating Market Changes

Understanding Market Dynamics

In an ever-evolving marketplace, staying attuned to shifts in economic indicators, consumer behavior, and industry trends is imperative for the sustainability and growth of your LLC. Consider the market as a living entity—constantly moving and changing. Your ability to observe, interpret, and react to these changes is crucial. Engaging regularly with market research reports, industry news, and economic forecasts provides a wealth of information. Utilizing tools like SWOT

(Strengths, Weaknesses, Opportunities, Threats) analysis can help you evaluate how external changes might impact your business and guide strategic decision-making.

Additionally, attending industry conferences and networking events offers dual benefits: gaining firsthand insights into market trends and fostering relationships that could lead to collaborative opportunities. Engaging with professionals in your field allows you to gauge the market's pulse, providing a clearer picture of emerging patterns that could affect your business. By embedding these practices into your routine, you ensure that your business adapts and thrives in changing conditions.

Leveraging Competitive Intelligence

Competitive intelligence is your secret weapon in predicting and responding to market movements. By systematically gathering and analyzing data about your competitors, you can anticipate their next moves, identify market gaps, and refine your strategies to maintain a competitive edge. Start by identifying key competitors and monitoring their activities, including product launches, marketing campaigns, and customer feedback. Tools like Google Alerts and social media monitoring platforms can automate this process, providing real-time updates on competitor behavior.

However, the true power of competitive intelligence lies in its application. Use the insights gathered to anticipate market shifts—such as a competitor entering a new segment—and adjust your strategies accordingly. For instance, if a competitor's pricing strategy reveals an underserved market tier, consider adjusting your pricing or value proposition to capture this segment. The goal is to transform collected data into actionable intelligence that propels your business forward.

Scenario Planning Techniques

Scenario planning is an invaluable technique in your strategic arsenal, allowing you to visualize different future scenarios and prepare appropriate responses. This method involves identifying key factors that could impact your business—from economic conditions to technological advancements—and imagining plausible future states based on these factors. For each scenario, develop a robust plan addressing potential challenges and leveraging opportunities.

To implement scenario planning effectively, start brainstorming with your team about possible future events that could impact your business, both positively and negatively. Develop detailed scenarios for each and explore how your business would respond. This exercise prepares you for potential future events and enhances your strategic thinking and agility. By regularly updating and revisiting your scenarios, you ensure that your business remains responsive and adaptable to whatever the future holds.

Adapting to Market Needs

In a marketplace where change is the only constant, flexibility and responsiveness are key to survival and success. This means not only keeping up with market changes but also being prepared to pivot your strategies as needed. Diversifying product lines, modifying pricing strategies, and refining marketing approaches are critical maneuvers that may need to be employed swiftly in response to changing market dynamics.

For instance, consider the impact of shifting consumer preferences on your product offerings. If market research indicates a growing demand for sustainable products in your industry, adapting your product line to include eco-friendly options could capture this emerging market segment and differentiate your business from competitors. Similarly, pricing strategies may need adjustment in response to economic downturns or shifts in consumer spending behavior, ensuring your products remain attractive and competitive.

By maintaining a flexible approach and staying attuned to market needs, you can navigate changes effectively and keep your business aligned with customer expectations and market realities. Implementing regular reviews of your business strategy, involving key team members in these reviews, and being willing to make courageous strategic shifts will empower your business to thrive in a dynamic market environment.

Innovations in Business Technology and Their Implementation

In this fast-paced digital era, staying abreast of technological advancements is essential for securing a competitive edge and fostering long-term sustainability in your business. Technologies such as artificial intelligence (AI), blockchain, and the Internet of Things (IoT) are transformative tools that can significantly enhance operational efficiency, customer experience, and market reach. This chapter explores how you can identify and integrate these technologies into your business to drive growth and innovation.

Identifying Relevant Technologies

Navigating the vast landscape of emerging technologies can seem daunting. Each industry has unique needs and challenges, and the technology that revolutionizes one sector may not be relevant in another. Start by clearly defining the problems you need to solve or the processes you want to enhance. For instance, if customer data security is a concern, blockchain technology could provide a robust solution with its enhanced security features. If improving operational efficiency is your goal, AI-driven automation tools could streamline processes, reduce human error, and free up your team for more strategic tasks.

Conducting a thorough analysis of your industry's technology trends is crucial. This can involve engaging with industry reports, attending technology expos, and participating in relevant webinars and workshops. Networking with peers and technology experts can provide insights into what technologies are gaining traction in your sector. Remember, the goal is not just to jump on the latest tech bandwagon but to choose technologies that align with your business objectives and offer tangible benefits.

Assessing Technology Impact

Once you've pinpointed potential technologies, the next step is to assess their impact on your business operations. This assessment should be meticulous and data-driven, involving a detailed cost-benefit analysis and estimation of return on investment (ROI). Start by cataloging the costs associated with implementing the new technology, including initial investment, training, integration, and ongoing maintenance. Then, evaluate the potential benefits. For AI implementations, benefits might include increased speed of service, reduced operational costs, and improved customer satisfaction.

Calculating ROI is pivotal here. Compare the expected benefits (e.g., increased revenue, cost savings) with the costs over a specific period. This analysis not only helps in making informed decisions but also sets realistic expectations for stakeholders. It's wise to consider the scalability of the technology—can it grow and evolve with your business? The best technological investments are those that address immediate needs while offering long-term utility.

Strategies for Technology Adoption

Adopting new technology involves more than just financial investment; it requires a strategic approach to integration and user adoption. Begin with pilot testing—a controlled method of evaluating the new technology on a smaller scale before a full rollout. This approach allows you to identify potential issues and make necessary adjustments without disrupting your entire operation. Select a segment of your business operations that would benefit most from the technology and monitor the results closely.

Training and support are crucial for successful technology adoption. Invest in comprehensive training programs to ensure your team is proficient in using the new tools. This might involve on-site training sessions, online courses, or hiring specialists for in-depth workshops.

Additionally, consider the user-friendliness of the technology—solutions that are intuitive and easy to use are more likely to be embraced by your team.

Integration with existing systems is another critical aspect. The new technology should seamlessly integrate with your current operations and software solutions. This may require customizations or consulting with IT professionals to ensure compatibility and optimize functionality.

Staying Informed on Tech Trends

In the realm of technology, change is the only constant. Maintaining a proactive approach to learning and staying updated on new advancements can position your business as a leader rather than a follower. Dedicate time regularly to read industry publications, attend tech seminars, and participate in relevant online communities to stay informed about the latest developments. Encourage your team to engage in continuous learning; consider setting up a learning fund or offering incentives for completing technology-focused courses and certifications.

Attending global technology conferences can also be immensely beneficial. These events provide insights into emerging technologies and opportunities to observe how other businesses implement new tools and solutions. Moreover, these gatherings are excellent for networking with tech innovators and peers who can provide new perspectives and inspire innovative ideas.

By actively engaging with the technological landscape, carefully assessing potential impacts, strategically adopting new tools, and fostering a culture of continuous learning, you empower your business to thrive in this digital age. These practices enhance your operational capabilities and ensure your business remains adaptive and forward-thinking in a world where technological evolution is relentless.

Long-Term Strategic Planning for Your LLC

Developing a Vision for the Future

Envisioning the future of your LLC is more than a mere exercise in creativity; it is about grounding your aspirations in a vision that guides every strategic decision you make. This vision serves as a lighthouse, helping to navigate your business through the turbulent waters of the market. Begin by imagining where you want your business to be in the next 5, 10, or even 20 years. What does success look like for you? Is it about expanding your market reach, innovating new products, or perhaps influencing your industry?

Crafting a clear and compelling vision involves deep introspection and forward-thinking. It encompasses not only your end goals but also the values that define your business's path. These core principles will guide your business's behavior and decisions, creating a consistent experience for both employees and customers. As you articulate this vision, consider the impact you want your business to have on the world. This might include leading in sustainability practices, being at the forefront of technological advancements, or setting new standards in customer service.

Once your vision is defined, communicate it effectively throughout your organization. This clarity ensures that every team member understands and shares in this vision, aligning their efforts towards common goals. It transforms abstract concepts into a shared ethos that motivates and drives your organization forward. Remember, a vision without action remains an illusion, so the next step is to set actionable goals to turn this vision into reality.

Setting Long-Term Goals

With your vision clearly defined, the next step is to translate this into strategic long-term goals. These are not just any goals; they are specifically designed to propel your business toward the future you envision. Start by identifying broad objectives that align with your vision, then break these down into more specific, measurable, and time-bound goals. For instance, if your vision includes leading in environmental sustainability, a long-term goal might be to reduce your operational carbon footprint by 50% within ten years.

Each goal should come with a set of actionable objectives and clear milestones. This breakdown not only makes the goal more manageable but also allows for tracking progress and making adjustments as needed. It's crucial to embed flexibility into this process, allowing your strategy to evolve in response to changes in the business environment or new opportunities that arise. Regularly revisiting and revising your long-term goals ensures they remain relevant and aligned with your overarching vision.

Engage your team in the goal-setting process. This inclusion fosters a sense of ownership and commitment while leveraging diverse perspectives that can enrich the strategy. Additionally, consider the resources—financial, human, and technological—that will be required to achieve these goals. Planning for these resources in advance can prevent bottlenecks down the road and ensure a smooth path toward your objectives.

Building a Sustainable Business Model

A sustainable business model goes beyond profitability; it integrates social, environmental, and economic elements into the core of your business operations. This approach not only ensures the long-term viability of your business but also responds to the growing consumer and stakeholder demand for responsible business practices. Start by assessing the impact of your business activities on the environment and community. Identify areas where your business can reduce waste, conserve resources, and enhance community well-being.

Implementing sustainable practices might involve adopting green technologies, reducing emissions, or ensuring fair labor practices across your supply chain. Each of these actions contributes to a more sustainable planet and enhances your business's reputation and appeal to eco-conscious consumers and employees.

Financial sustainability is equally important. This involves establishing strong financial controls, diversifying income streams, and planning for economic fluctuations. A robust financial foundation enables you to invest in innovation and growth initiatives without jeopardizing your business's stability.

Succession Planning and Legacy Building

Finally, consider the legacy you wish to leave through your business. Succession planning is critical to ensuring that your business thrives beyond your direct involvement, whether due to retirement, health issues, or other reasons. Begin by identifying potential leaders within your organization who can take over management roles in the future. Invest in their development through training programs, mentorship, and leadership opportunities.

Documenting processes and best practices is also part of this legacy-building effort. This documentation ensures that the business can continue to operate smoothly without your constant input and maintains the quality and standards you've set. Additionally, consider the legal and financial aspects of succession, including ownership transfer and estate planning, to avoid potential disputes and ensure a smooth transition.

Through thoughtful long-term strategic planning, you can steer your LLC toward a future that not only meets your financial goals but also aligns with your personal values and aspirations. This process is about building a business that lasts, contributes positively to society, and leaves a lasting legacy.

Brief Ending to the Chapter

In this chapter, we explored the critical elements of strategic planning that will prepare your LLC for the future. From developing a clear vision to setting actionable goals, building a sustainable business model, and planning for succession, each step is designed to ensure your business not only survives but thrives in the years to come. As we move forward, remember that the strategies outlined here are not static; they require adaptability and ongoing evaluation to remain effective. Let's carry these insights into the next chapter, where we will delve into enhancing operational efficiencies and fostering a culture of innovation.

CONCLUSION

As we draw the curtain on this comprehensive journey through the intricate yet fulfilling process of starting and managing your LLC, take a moment to reflect on the significant strides you've made by navigating these pages. From laying the groundwork and understanding the legalities to mastering financial management and exploring growth strategies, you now possess the toolkit to navigate the exciting world of entrepreneurship.

Key Takeaways for Your Entrepreneurial Journey

Remember, the core of your success lies in meticulous planning, understanding your market, and adapting to the ever-evolving legal and financial landscapes. The steps outlined—selecting a business name, registering your LLC, complying with legal standards, managing finances, and scaling your business—are not just tasks but milestones that pave the path toward your entrepreneurial independence.

The Empowerment of Entrepreneurship

Owning an LLC transcends mere business transactions; it is a journey toward independence and empowerment. This path allows you to craft your destiny, make decisions that align with your values, and impact your community in meaningful ways. The autonomy to steer your business in alignment with your personal and professional goals is one of the most rewarding aspects of entrepreneurship.

The Imperative of Continuous Learning and Adaptation

The business landscape is perpetually changing, and staying informed is key to your continued success. Embrace the practice of continuous learning and remain adaptable to new information and technologies. This agility will not only safeguard your business against unforeseen challenges but also open doors to innovative opportunities.

A Call to Action: Dive In and Drive Forward

Now, with the knowledge and insights gained, it's time to take that bold step forward. Implement the strategies discussed, leverage your newfound skills, and start making a difference with your LLC. Remember, the world of business waits for no one and rewards those who dive in with determination and persistence.

Gratitude and Encouragement

I am incredibly grateful that you chose to embark on this journey with this guide as your companion. Thank you for investing your time and trust in these pages. As you move forward, remember that every challenge is an opportunity for growth and every success is a stepping stone to greater achievements. Approach each day with resilience and optimism.

Personal Reflection

Reflecting on my own journey as an entrepreneur and small business manager, I understand the hurdles and high points you might encounter. Sharing them with you has not only been a privilege but a profound reminder of our shared aspirations and challenges.

As you turn these insights into action, know that you are not alone. The community of entrepreneurs is vibrant and supportive. Reach out, engage, and continue to share your experiences. Together, we thrive in a network of innovation, support, and collective growth.

Here's to your success as you forge ahead, building a business that reflects your passion, meets your financial goals, and brings positive change. Let's continue to grow, inspire, and lead with courage and creativity.

REFERENCES

Harvard Business School Online. (n.d.). *How to conduct market research for a startup*. Harvard Business School Online. https://online.hbs.edu/blog/post/how-to-do-market-research-for-a-startup

NerdWallet. (n.d.). *LLC vs. corporation: Which is right for your business?* NerdWallet. https://www.nerdwallet.com/article/small-business/llc-vs-corporation

Collective. (n.d.). *How to start an LLC for all 50 states guide*. Collective. https://www.collective.com/guides/how-to-start-an-llc-for-all-50-states

U.S. Small Business Administration. (n.d.). *Write your business plan*. U.S. Small Business Administration. https://www.sba.gov/business-guide/plan-your-business/write-your-business-plan

Forbes. (n.d.). *LLC name requirements, ideas & examples*. Forbes. https://www.forbes.com/advisor/business/llc-names/

FindLaw. (n.d.). *How to write and file the articles of organization for your LLC*. FindLaw. https://www.findlaw.com/smallbusiness/incorporation-and-legal-structures/forming-an-llc-writing-and-filing-the-articles-of-organization.html

Forbes. (n.d.). *What is a registered agent for an LLC & do you need one?* Forbes. https://www.forbes.com/advisor/business/what-is-registered-agent/#:~:text=Hiring%20a%20professional%20registered%20agent,%2450%20and%20%24300%20per%20year.

American Bar Association. (n.d.). *LLC agreement checklist.* American Bar Association. https://www.americanbar.org/groups/gpsolo/resources/ereport/archive/llc-agreement-checklist/

FasterCapital. (n.d.). *The pros and cons of bootstrapping vs seeking investment for your startup.* FasterCapital. https://fastercapital.com/content/The-pros-and-cons-of-bootstrapping-vs-seeking-investment-for-your-startup.html

Finmark. (n.d.). *How to pitch investors: 14 tips to get your startup funded.* Finmark. https://finmark.com/how-to-pitch-investors/

SmartAsset. (n.d.). *What are the tax benefits of an LLC?* SmartAsset. https://smartasset.com/taxes/what-are-the-tax-benefits-of-an-llc

PCMag. (2024). *The best accounting software for small businesses in 2024.* PCMag. https://www.pcmag.com/picks/the-best-small-business-accounting-software

Nolo. (n.d.). *State guide to LLC report and tax filing requirements.* Nolo. https://www.nolo.com/legal-encyclopedia/50-state-guide-annual-report-tax-filing-requirements-llcs

LegalZoom. (n.d.). *A checklist for maintaining your corporate veil.* LegalZoom. https://www.legalzoom.com/articles/a-checklist-for-maintaining-your-corporate-veil

U.S. Chamber of Commerce. (n.d.). *What every small business should know about intellectual property.* U.S. Chamber of Commerce. https://www.uschamber.com/co/start/strategy/intellectual-property-what-small-businesses-should-know

Forbes. (n.d.). *Mediation vs. arbitration: Differences, pros, cons.* Forbes. https://www.forbes.com/advisor/legal/mediation-vs-arbitration/

Reliablesoft. (n.d.). *Digital marketing for startups (complete guide).* Reliablesoft. https://www.reliablesoft.net/digital-marketing-for-startups/

Northwest Registered Agent. (n.d.). *Hiring employees as an LLC.* Northwest Registered Agent. https://www.northwestregisteredagent.com/llc/hiring-employees

Business News Daily. (n.d.). *Customer retention strategies for small businesses.* Business News Daily. https://www.businessnewsdaily.com/5833-how-to-keep-customers.html

U.S. Chamber of Commerce. (n.d.). *Examining the impact of technology on small businesses.* U.S. Chamber of Commerce. https://www.uschamber.com/assets/archived/images/ctec_sme-rpt_v3.pdf

Thomson Reuters. (n.d.). *How are LLCs taxed? LLC tax benefits and ways to reduce taxes.* Thomson Reuters. https://tax.thomsonreuters.com/blog/how-are-llcs-taxed-llc-tax-benefits-and-tips-to-reduce-taxes/

Bank of America. (n.d.). *How to manage cash flow for your business.* Bank of America. https://business.bankofamerica.com/resources/cash-flow-management-basics-for-small-businesses.html

LinkedIn. (n.d.). *A comprehensive guide to securing venture capital funding for your startup.* LinkedIn. https://www.linkedin.com/pulse/comprehensive-guide-securing-venture-capital-funding-your-wspbe

BNY Mellon Wealth Management. (n.d.). *Eight steps to an effective business transition.* BNY Mellon Wealth Management. https://www.bnymellonwealth.com/insights/eight-steps-to-an-effective-business-transition.html

Fine Point Consulting. (n.d.). *8 financial challenges for startups & early-stage businesses.* Fine Point Consulting. https://www.finepointconsulting.com/post/8-common-financial-challenges-for-startups-and-early-stage-businesses

Forbes. (2024). *15 effective employee retention strategies in 2024.* Forbes. https://www.forbes.com/advisor/business/employee-retention-strategies/

PR Lab. (n.d.). *21 effective crisis management plan examples.* PR Lab. https://prlab.co/blog/21-effective-crisis-management-plan-examples/

Zapier. (2024). *The 9 best competitor analysis tools in 2024.* Zapier. https://zapier.com/blog/competitor-analysis-tools/

Forbes. (2024). *Best e-commerce platforms for small business in 2024.* Forbes. https://www.forbes.com/advisor/business/software/best-ecommerce-platform/

Trade.gov. (n.d.). *Comply with U.S. and foreign regulations.* Trade.gov. https://www.trade.gov/comply-us-and-foreign-regulations

Harvard Business School Online. (n.d.). *The importance of sustainability in business.* Harvard Business School Online. https://online.hbs.edu/blog/post/business-sustainability-strategies

LegalZoom. (n.d.). *How to franchise your business: 7 steps for small businesses.* LegalZoom. https://www.legalzoom.com/articles/how-to-franchise-your-business-7-steps-for-small-businesses

MasterClass. (2024). *How to build a memorable brand in 6 steps.* MasterClass. https://www.masterclass.com/articles/how-to-build-a-memorable-brand

ZenMedia. (n.d.). *19 successful PR campaigns and why they worked.* ZenMedia. https://zenmedia.com/blog/9-successful-pr-campaigns/

Sprout Social. (n.d.). *How to build your social media marketing strategy.* Sprout Social. https://sproutsocial.com/insights/social-media-marketing-strategy/

Harvard Business Review. (2017). *Why your company culture should match your brand.* Harvard Business Review. https://hbr.org/2017/06/why-your-company-culture-should-match-your-brand

Forbes. (2022). *The 5 biggest business trends in 2023 everyone must get right.* Forbes. https://www.forbes.com/sites/bernardmarr/2022/10/03/the-5-biggest-business-trends-for-2023/

SEMrush. (n.d.). *Competitive intelligence: What it is & how to gather it.* SEMrush. https://www.semrush.com/blog/competitive-intelligence/

Forbes. (2023). *How artificial intelligence is helping today's small businesses.* Forbes. https://www.forbes.com/sites/charlesrtaylor/2023/08/09/how-artificial-intelligence-is-helping-todays-small-businesses/

Indeed. (n.d.). *How to create a long-term strategy in 8 steps.* Indeed. https://www.indeed.com/career-advice/career-development/long-term-strategy

9 7 9 8 9 9 9 0 7 3 4 9 0 6